IMAGES
of America

CHIMNEY ROCK
NATIONAL
MONUMENT

The Chimney Rock National Monument is replete with history, conjecture, and adventure, providing an opportunity to view a culture's innovative response to an interesting and dynamic geographic location. This aerial view dramatizes the Chimney Rock Great House atop the cuesta, with the pinnacles of Companion Rock and Chimney Rock in the background. (Courtesy of US Forest Service, Pagosa District.)

ON THE COVER: Adventurous local families traveled through difficult terrain to visit the ruins and pinnacles of Chimney Rosa Mesa. Here, three locals rest on a rock outcropping with Companion Rock in the foreground and Chimney Rock in the background. (Courtesy of Laura Whitt.)

IMAGES
of America

CHIMNEY ROCK
NATIONAL
MONUMENT

Amron Gravett and Christine Robinette
Foreword By Glenn Raby

ARCADIA
PUBLISHING

Copyright © 2014 by Amron Gravett and Christine Robinette
ISBN 978-1-4671-3161-2

Published by Arcadia Publishing
Charleston, South Carolina

Printed in the United States of America

Library of Congress Control Number: 2013957661

For all general information, please contact Arcadia Publishing:
Telephone 843-853-2070
Fax 843-853-0044
E-mail sales@arcadiapublishing.com
For customer service and orders:
Toll-Free 1-888-313-2665

Visit us on the Internet at www.arcadiapublishing.com

*To the people of the Southwest, past, present, and future, may you
continue to treasure the history and culture of this grand landscape.*

CONTENTS

FOREWORD

Chimney Rock is a small dot on the vast Colorado Plateau—two sandstone pillars stand atop a sloping ridge at the center of a ring of mountains. A river cuts through this shallow bowl, washing the western base of the ridge. It is just a few thousand acres, not much more than six square miles of land. Yet, this little patch of ground may once have been as important to the people of the southwestern United States as the Royal Observatory, Greenwich is to today's world.

Chimney Rock is a rarity among national monuments—a place where nature has created a perfect theater to showcase the beauty of the skies and the cycles of the sun and moon. The site not only frames the two most commanding objects in the sky during their most significant moments, but also provides the ideal place from which to view these spectacles. It is almost as if a stage were set for the eyes and minds that would someday come to observe and wonder.

The first people to gaze up at Chimney Rock must have been struck by its unique beauty and wondered about its meaning. No one knows when its link to the cycles of the sun and especially the moon were discovered, but by the mid-11th century, this connection had brought the Ancestral Puebloans of the Chaco culture here. Did they revere the rocks as predictors of the future, as Nature's grand clock, as a way to know their world? They left no written testimony, only enticing clues. However, it is almost incomprehensible that they did not feel the awe that we today feel when we watch the full moon rise between the rock pillars during the winter solstice.

Like those past peoples, we are only here for a brief time, only temporary stewards of this inspiring place. We are just one moment in Chimney Rock's history. We owe it to the world and the future not to lose or destroy that history.

—Glenn Raby

Acknowledgments

It is with appreciation that we acknowledge the important persons that have aided in the research and compilation of this book. Thank you, to the archaeologists of past and present, who have worked under sometimes extreme weather conditions to protect these important, irreplaceable cultural resources. Thank you, to the scholars and historians who have uncovered, interpreted, and shared their understanding of the region's people and landmarks. We have named them throughout the book where their research and ideas are relevant.

Thank you, to the countless volunteers of the early and present-day steward groups, including the Chimney Rock Interpretive Association (CRIA) for their years of dedication to preserving the history and access of Chimney Rock. A special thank-you goes to CRIA members Shelleah Conitchan, Tanice Rampsberger, Helen Richardson, and Lyniss Steinert; to US Forest Service employees Julie Coleman, Mark Roper, and Wendy Sutton; to Anasazi Heritage Center's Tracy Murphy; to Cory Breternitz, David Kinder, Greg Munson, Brandon Oberhardt, Glenn Raby, Clint Swink, and Laura Whitt; and a huge thank-you goes to Maia Banks and Matt Gravett.

The following collections were utilized during the researching of this book: Anasazi Heritage Center, Archaeology Southwest, Center for Southwest Studies and Reed Library (Fort Lewis College), Chaco Research Archive, Durango Herald, Durango Public Library, History Colorado, Laboratory of Anthropology (Museum of Indian Arts and Culture), Ruby Sisson Memorial Library, San Juan Historical Society Museum, School for Advanced Research, University of Colorado at Boulder, University of Denver, US Forest Service, US Geological Survey, and US National Park Service. As librarians and researchers, we value the preservation of our historical record in digital format made both searchable and accessible to the public free of charge.

Chimney Rock National Monument is not intended to be a comprehensive history of the Chimney Rock area. Rather, it is a photographic glimpse of the many persons, sites, and preservation efforts that this unique landmark has observed over the last 100 years. If you are looking for more detailed information, we encourage you to explore the valuable resources in the above collections, as well as those listed in the bibliography.

INTRODUCTION

On the autumnal equinox, September 21, 2012, President Obama signed a proclamation creating the Chimney Rock National Monument. The US Forest Service collaborated with tribal, community, federal, and state partners to enact the legislation necessary to manifest the protection of this unique historic, cultural, and educational site.

The Chimney Rock National Monument encompasses 4,726 acres of the San Juan National Forest. The care of the cultural resources of Chimney Rock and Peterson Mesa has been placed under the management of the US Forest Service (USFS) in collaboration with the Chimney Rock Interpretive Association (CRIA) and tribal partners.

Located in the southwest corner of Colorado, the mesa with protruding Chimney Rock and Companion Rock watches over profound architectural dwellings and buildings of the Ancestral Puebloans.

Geological evidence indicates the spires were formed 100,000 years ago when a vast inland sea retreated, followed by intense volcanic eruptions and a glaciation. The glaciers receded around 12,000 years ago and allowed human exploration (leading the early Native Americans to a fertile valley capable of sustaining people).

Understanding Chimney Rock's connection with Chaco Canyon has been the foundation of archaeological interpretations since the first official dig in 1921. There are nearly 200 known outlier communities of Chaco Canyon, all characterized by similar artifacts: a Great House, Great Kiva, and roads connected to Chaco. The great houses are planned structures complete with architectural symmetry and enclosed kivas. The location of the Chimney Rock Great House suggests both defensive and ceremonial purposes. Commerce between the outliers of Chacoan culture and Chaco Canyon itself is evidenced. It may have been used as a timber camp, hunting base, ceremonial center, or astronomical observatory (amongst other reasons).

The Chacoans used astronomical markers to orient the major lunar standstill between the two pinnacles. Today, as in times past, the moon rises between the two towers at its northernmost transit. The lunar standstills in 1076 and 1093 coincided with construction of the Great House pueblo atop the mesa. Watching the sky was important—the Chacoans were likely able to predict the summer and winter solstices and the fall and spring equinoxes. The Crab Nebula supernova of 1054 would have had a powerful effect on the sky watchers as well.

The Chacoan innovative period at Chimney Rock was from 900 to 1150. Prior to the Chacoan era, the San Juan River Basin was home to a number of inhabitants. They lived along the San Juan River, Stollsteimer Creek, and the Piedra River. They probably spoke different languages from the Chacoans. They were an available resource to the Chacoans— providing assistance in building the dwellings —and may have participated in ceremonies. These locals lived in proximity to the Chacoans and were likely greatly influenced by them.

There are many questions as to the departure of these peoples, but it is theorized that those who were here are the ancestors of the Pueblo peoples that are scattered through the Southwest. Hopi,

Taos, Zuni, and other Puebloans consider Chimney Rock as a place of origin, and some continue to hold ceremonies here. For the past few decades, stewards of Chimney Rock have consulted with a council of 26 tribes to provide management and resource use guidance.

This site has attracted anthropologists from the early 1920s to the present. The architecture, artifacts, and evidence of life lived here have brought explorers to uncover some of the 200 sites that are located around the mesa. Most research has been on the excavations of the dwellings at the top of the mesa, and includes the Great Kivas and Pit House site on the Lower Mesa, the Ridge House, the Guard House, and the Great Pueblo on the Upper Mesa (7,600 feet in elevation). A great many anthropologists, archaeologists, and scholars have contributed to our understanding of Chimney Rock's importance and history. They are referred to throughout this book.

In the 1920s, local residents visited this site on foot and by horseback before the roads were paved. The main road that exists today provides access to the visitor center and the upper parking lot.

Mystery writers have used the history and terrain of Chimney Rock to provide settings for their books. Unable to resist the vistas, photographers and artists throughout time have captured the landscape as well.

There are a variety of recreational activities allowed at the Chimney Rock National Monument. Some of those include archaeological visitation, astronomical and geological special events, cross-country skiing, hiking, mountain biking, and snowshoeing.

CRIA and its earlier manifestations have been a dynamic force in bringing this treasure to public notice. For over 40 years, dedicated volunteers have joined archaeological researchers in caring for this site and worked to make it available to the public for educational and inspirational knowledge. With the recent national monument proclamation, the USFS and CRIA are working with local groups in efforts to offer new and dynamic ways to serve the public in the appreciation of this remarkable manifestation of natural and human innovation.

Tours and additional information regarding the Chimney Rock National Monument can be accessed online at www.chimneyrockco.org.

Time Line of Significant Events at Chimney Rock

700–850: Ancestral Puebloans migrated into the region

950: First phase of building construction along Chimney Rock Mesa

1054: Crab Nebula supernova visible in the sky for more than three weeks and recorded as petroglyphs around the Southwest

1064: Sunset Crater—near Flagstaff, Arizona—erupted and was likely seen for hundreds of miles

1073–1077: Major lunar standstill when the moon rose between Companion Rock and Chimney Rock, evidence of Great House construction

1094: Major lunar standstill and additional Great House construction

1097: Total solar eclipse seen for four daylight minutes

1111: Major lunar standstill took place

1125–1150: Population decline and eventual abandonment of the Chimney Rock Mesa dwellings and surrounding valleys

1700s: Resettlement of region by people from the ancient Southwest regions

1921–1930: Various archaeological excavations at Chimney Rock performed by Jean Jeancon, Frank Roberts, and others—initially sponsored by the Colorado State Historical and Natural History Society and University of Denver

1943: First documented sighting of peregrine falcons by fire rangers stationed at Chimney Rock's Fire Lookout Tower

1970: Chimney Rock Archaeological Area listed in the National Register of Historic Places, which authorized protection of 960 acres

1970–1972: University of Colorado at Boulder archaeological crew—led by Frank Eddy—performed excavations and stabilization of some of the structures

1970s–1990s: Robert York, Sharon Hatch, and Gary Matlock—US Forest Service archaeologists—carried out experimental mortar work on Chimney Rock structures, sourcing local materials

1974: Site closed due to reoccupation of peregrine falcons nesting on rocks and their endangered species status

1978: Seasonal closure during peregrine falcon nesting season

1988: Peregrine falcon hacking project began

2004: Chimney Rock Interpretive Association awarded 501(c)(3) nonprofit status

2009: University of Colorado at Boulder archaeological crew—led by Stephen Lekson and Brenda Todd—performed work at the Great House. Woods Canyon Archaeological Consultants and Petrographics, both contractors, also supported the work.

2012: Chimney Rock National Monument proclaimed by Pres. Barack Obama under the authority of the Antiquities Act, which protected 4,726 acres of surrounding lands, including Peterson Mesa

2022: Next major lunar standstill to be witnessed at Chimney Rock National Monument

One

CHIMNEY ROCK'S MAGNIFICENCE
GEOGRAPHY AND GEOLOGY

Rising 1,000 feet above the Piedra River to a height of 7,600 feet are two spectacular pinnacles (high points in the terrain) reaching toward the skies. The dramatic geology of the monument stands in stark contrast to the majestic ponderosa pine forest and rolling savanna-like plains along the valley floor. The Piedra River cuts along the edge of Peterson Mesa in the western portion of the monument. Steep cliffs and expanses of exposed sandstone and shale are evidence of the geologic past.

The rocks surrounding the rock spires eroded from the once vast inland sea and left behind fossils in the sandstone. This was followed by volcanic eruptions and a glaciation period about 100,000 years ago. Glaciers retreated around 12,000 years ago and the climate warmed, thus allowing exploration of this fertile valley.

Since the retreat of the glaciers, abundant wildlife has flourished. Migratory mule deer and elk herds move through the area, as they have for thousands of years. Merriam's turkey and woodpeckers are supported by stands of piñon pine, juniper, mountain mahogany, mock orange, and Gambel oak. Ponderosa pine creates an overstory for a number of large animals, including mountain lions and bears. Eagles, ravens, and peregrine falcons nest at Chimney Rock. Several desert plants grow, including a variety of cholla cactus that does not naturally occur outside the Sonoran Desert and is believed to be associated with deliberate cultivation by the Ancestral Puebloans.

As a geologic landform, Chimney Rock has been a marker for travelers through the ages. When the function of the site as a celestial marker was first discovered, it became an important location to settle. Evidence suggests that there were numerous villages in the area and that over a thousand people lived there for a time. They farmed by utilizing the natural water flows that created silt deposits favorable to growing two strains of corn. Seventeen natural water catchments developed small ponds and lakes on this high mesa. The views the people experienced daily were spectacular. The night skies gave them information regarding the cycles of the seasons and the optimum dates for planting that would ensure their survival.

This land is old: 70 millions years old. Around 28 million years ago, a series of massive volcanic eruptions decimated life for hundreds of miles around the Four Corners and created a crater complex known as La Garita Caldera. At that time, the narrow rift of the Rio Grande Valley split the continent. Around 11,000 years ago, favorable climate conditions made travel over the passes

accessible. The San Juan Mountains completed their uplift and erosion began. In this panorama from the 1920s, the Piedra River cuts north-south along the Peterson Mesa formation. (Courtesy of BLM–Anasazi Heritage Center.)

The land of this Southwest plateau evokes a sense of mystery and wonder. On the left of this image, one sees the uplifting Peterson Mesa formation where it meets the Piedra River. Glaciers sculpted this landscape, thriving in conditions of cool, wet summers and icy winters. The rivers eroded valleys, depositing rock and sand into the San Juan River Basin. The ancient seabeds began to wear away, leaving exposed, thick sand layers that resisted any further erosion. Evidence of life in the Cretaceous inland seafloor can be seen in the ichnofossils of Ophiomorpha, which are found in the Pictured Cliffs Sandstone atop the mesa. (Courtesy of US Forest Service, Pagosa District.)

About 30,000 years ago, people inhabited this land with other large mammals, such as mammoths, mastodons, cave bears, saber-toothed tigers, dire wolves, and giant sloths. Slowly, humans began thriving as the dominator of the landscape. Throughout this period, the sandstone pillars stood high on the island mesa, contained by the waters of the Piedra River, Devil Creek, and Stollsteimer Creek. (Courtesy of US Forest Service, Pagosa District.)

The stone spires rise hundreds of feet above the Piedra River valley floor to an elevation of 7,600 feet. During the first archaeological expedition in 1921, Etienne Renaud wrote in his field journal, "The light sets in sharp relief the contour of the Chimney Rocks and their steep slopes." (Courtesy US Forest Service, Pagosa District.)

The geologic wonder of the twin spires is a naturally made landmark. Geologist and longtime Chimney Rock custodian Glenn Raby calls it a "sensitive landmark." The site is compelling to all who view it. Humans have responded to its energetic force for thousands of years. The top of Chimney Rock is made up of Pictured Cliffs Sandstone, while the base is made up of the Mesa Verde Group. (Courtesy of US Forest Service, Pagosa District.)

Engaged by the vision of this landmark, Spanish-speaking travelers once called it "La Piedra Parada." Tewa-speaking pueblos referred to it as "Fire Mountain," and other regional tribes view the pinnacles as stone manifestations of the Twin Warrior Gods. Visitors often remark about the faces seen in the rocks. In 1921, archaeologist Jean Jeancon named the spires Chimney and Companion Rocks. (Courtesy of Shelleah Conitchan.)

The Piedra River and Stollsteimer Creek contain gravel made up of chalcedony, flint, jasper, agate, limestone, granite, and volcanic rocks. This lithic medley provided early inhabitants clay and materials for tools and arrowheads. The future of the formations is as uncertain as that of mankind. These monoliths are likely to erode particle by particle, grain by grain, eventually being swept down the riverbeds to a home in the ocean floor. As writer Craig Childs describes the view, "The towers stood high in fading light, two dark, knobby monoliths eroded from the far end of the ridge." Local adventurers took these photographs in 1924. (Both, courtesy of Laura Whitt.)

Winter snow helped maintain a year-round water source for the settlements around the upper San Juan River Basin. The Medieval Warm Period (900–1300) was marked by climatic factors, such as elevated temperatures, floodplain variation, and increased droughts. Although climate conditions have changed over the course of time, several factors have remained steadfast, including water, sun, soil, and plant and animal life. These wintry photographs from 1979 (above) and 1984 (below) portray the excellent winter snow season that exists here at 6,000–7,000 feet in elevation. (Both, courtesy of US Forest Service, Pagosa District.)

The people of Chimney Rock likely used silver sage as a cleansing herb (it is still used today by people all over the Southwest). The wood was used for construction, weavings, and fuel. Leaves and seeds were eaten, and the camphor in them was used both medicinally and as a natural dye. (Courtesy of US Forest Service, Pagosa District.)

Dendrochronology is used to date the roofing beams found in prehistoric structures. Every year, a tree grows a ring of wood around its trunk. The unique patterns of these rings show evidence of fire damage and of wet and dry cycles. Using a library of tree ring samples, a cross section of wood is compared and the outermost tree ring corresponds to the date the tree died. (Courtesy of the authors' collection.)

In 1921, Etienne Renaud noted, "There are still some very tall pine trees in this region which used to be heavily forested. Many old log roads furrow the hills all around the camp. An important lumber camp, no longer active, was located a short distance below our camp [near Devil Creek on the north slope of Chimney Rock Mesa]." (Courtesy of the authors' collection.)

Chimney Rock has been called Chaco Canyon's logging town. Many interpreters think that massive ponderosa pines were cut, lashed together, and sent in rafts down the Piedra River to the San Juan River, eventually unloading the cargo near present-day Salmon Ruins in Bloomfield, New Mexico. There, the timber may have been transported along the Great North Road to the city center of Chaco Canyon. (Courtesy of the authors' collection.)

In 1974, a pair of peregrine falcons was found nesting on Companion Rock. At that time, they were protected under the Endangered Species Act and the area was closed. Volunteer observers began protecting and studying the site. Due to ingestion of DDT, the falcons produced fragile eggshells, thereby decreasing their populations to near extinction. Chimney Rock was one of only a handful of Colorado nesting sites for the raptors. Wildlife biologists successfully performed hatch replacement experiments, collecting eggs and raising them in controlled conditions (a method called hacking). Wildlife biologist Marcy Cottrell Houle writes of her experience as a peregrine protector during the 1970s in her book *Wings for My Flight*. Today, volunteers still protect the nesting grounds. (Above, courtesy of US Forest Service; left, courtesy of Pat Jackson.)

There have been a few pairs of peregrines, well known as raptors that mate for life, at Chimney Rock over the years. In 1978, the *Durango-Cortez Herald* published a heroic survival story about two Chimney Rock peregrines named King Arthur and Lady. The juvenile peregrine falcon in these photographs was found wounded near the Chimney Rock entrance by Helen Richardson and Cher Logsdon—two volunteers from Chimney Rock Interpretive Association—in 2011. These photographs show Pat Jackson holding the peregrine, nicknamed "Pinnacle," at the nearby St. Francis Wildlife Rehabilitation Center. While in rehabilitation, Pinnacle's female partner waited for him for two months until he was successfully released with a healthy wing. (Right, courtesy of the authors' collection; below, courtesy of Sandy Billings.)

The mystical spires have intrigued people for over a thousand years. For the past hundred years, tourism promoters have used the spires' geology, geography, and cultural remains as a lure to bring travelers to the mesa. The number of archaeological and cultural sites in the Four Corners region draws visitors to explore and investigate the wonder that is the Southwest. (Courtesy of the authors' collection.)

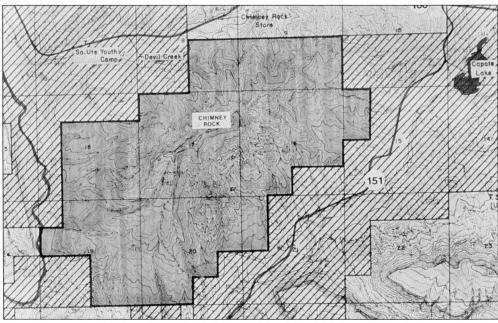

The Chimney Rock National Monument includes 4,726 acres (over six square miles) within Archuleta County. This 1983 US Forest Service map shows the shaded boundaries of the Chimney Rock Archaeological Area, which encompassed over 3,000 acres at that time. One of the significant additions from 1983 to 2012 was the inclusion of the Peterson Mesa archaeological sites. (Courtesy of US Forest Service, Pagosa District.)

The earliest inhabitants of the area were the Ancestral Puebloans (who built the Chimney Rock structures), and then later the Apache, Navajo, and Utes. French and Spanish explorers visited the area in the 1600–1700s, and some remained and settled communities along the rivers. The Brunot Treaty of 1873–1874 established the Southern Ute Reservation at its present location. By 1881, the Denver & Rio Grande Railroad arrived and helped establish the larger towns within Archuleta County. Geographic landmarks showcase this ethnically diverse history by some of their names: Pagosa (Ute for "boiling water"), Indian Creek Divide and Navajo Peak, Arboles (Spanish for "trees"), Cabezon Canyon (Spanish for "head"), and Piedra Parada (Spanish for "standing stone" and an early name for Chimney Rock). Shown here are two early US Forest Service panoramas taken from the Chimney Rock Fire Lookout Tower. (Both, courtesy of BLM–Anasazi Heritage Center.)

Chimney Rock National Monument is located in a very distinct and remote area of southwestern Colorado. Today, it is within Archuleta County. The county includes 1,355 square miles, 50 percent of which are in the San Juan National Forest. Archuleta County is named in honor of Antonio Archuleta, a senator from Conejos County (which was divided to create Archuleta County in 1885). In 1859, US Army captain John Macomb reported, "The Piedra Parada, a well-known landmark, which has conferred its name upon the Rio Piedra, is a chimney-like column of rock, rising with its base to the height of eight or nine hundred feet above the surrounding country." This August 1948 photograph showcases the precipice of the mesa and the pinnacles' prominence, with Companion Rock (foreground) and Chimney Rock (background). (Courtesy of BLM–Anasazi Heritage Center.)

Two

LIVING ON THE LAND
THEN AND NOW

Diverse groups have existed for over a thousand years in this region. The people once called the Anasazi, meaning "ancient enemy" or "ancient ones" in Navajo, are referred to today as Ancestral Puebloans. They found life to be sustainable along the Piedra and San Juan Rivers, and the settlements here were in place when the Chacoans realized that Chimney Rock was a celestial marker location. The local dwellers likely became labor resources for building the structures on the top of the mesa. It is believed that although they spoke different languages, they were still able to share their knowledge. One may wonder how the children were raised in such a perilous location. The precipices adjacent to the pit house are steep and hazardous to any curious child. They must have learned at an early age to navigate carefully.

Because the people mastered storage, food was abundant and readily available. Their understanding of the chemistry needed to make pottery demonstrates not only their intelligence, but also the human capacity for invention and design. Though life must have been hard, it must also have been filled with the pleasures of amazing sunrises and sunsets.

Due to the changes in climate, the plant community that grows here now may be different from flora during earlier times. There is controversy about whether the people collected piñon nuts (although people savor them today). The ponderosa pine trees, as well as other plants, were here then and remain today. Elk, deer, bears, and birds provided the people sustenance and played an important role in their survival and worldview.

From the 360-degree vistas of the rivers and mountains that encircle the spires, visitors watch peregrine falcons swoop and dive while ravens perch in the 400-year-old piñon and juniper trees. Visitors can climb to the top of the cuesta to observe the lunar events and even attend occasional classes on Ancestral Puebloan techniques for creating pottery and utensils. Visitors leave this monument with a respect for the creativity and skills needed to live here and the labor employed to build dwellings in such a lofty location.

People have lived in the region known as the upper San Juan River Basin for over a thousand years. The environment has sustained people and animal populations alike with its plentiful game, fish, edible plants, and water. Here, a cowboy displays his catch from nearby Devil Creek while gazing south to Chimney and Companion Rocks. Charles Beise (1909–1983) of the Denver Museum of Natural History likely took this 1941 photograph on Earl Ford's ranch while visiting the area. In 1941, Beise exhibited his wild turkey action shots at the Pennington Studio in Durango. The ponderosa pine tree in the foreground showcases one of the most prominent evergreens of the San Juan National Forest; it is still seen in abundance and managed by the USFS today. (Courtesy of US Forest Service, Pagosa District.)

Dwarfed by the monolith, five climbers ascend Chimney Rock on June 1, 1940. According to the *Durango Herald-Democrat*, Elwyn Arps, Carl Blaurock, Lewis Giesecke, Walter Prager, and Betty Turner scaled the chimney and built a cairn that could be seen from US Highway 160. Turner recalled, "I can do most any kind of dance, ride most any kind of horse, but when it comes to swinging out over an overhanging rock with only a little old rope to hang to, and a landing place so far below, I still stick to dancing or horses." The *Herald-Democrat* reported that they were the first known to reach the summit and that the climb "was unusually hazardous as the rock was rotten." (Both, courtesy of US Forest Service, Pagosa District.)

The Chimney Rock Cafe sits along Devil Creek, US Highway 160, and the northern base of the pinnacles—a route earlier known as the Spanish Trail. Since 1920, there has been a restaurant and/or general store there. Over the years, it has supported travelers on foot, by car, and even those passing through by horse. Various owners have operated it over the years, including Bradley Cooper in the 1940s. It is still in operation today and includes a restaurant, tavern, RV park, and wild game processing. (Above, courtesy of US Forest Service, Pagosa District; below, courtesy of the authors' collection.)

On October 31, 1950, Mabel Cooper was postmistress when the town name was officially changed from Dyke to Chimney Rock, Colorado. In commemoration of the event, Cooper received 159 requests from stamp collectors to mail off stamped postage with old and new town stamps. Nested inside the Chimney Rock Store, the post office served several hundred people. (Courtesy of US Forest Service, Pagosa District.)

Today, Rafter T Ranch is located along the Piedra River where the Pargin and Harlan families ranched. In 1921, Etienne Renaud noted, "Mounds and indications of pit houses were pretty abundant . . . They begin about where this road turns from Devils Creek to the Piedra upstream, by the Pargin Ranch, in the neighborhood of the Schoolhouses as far at least as in front of the Piedra P.O." (Courtesy of the authors' collection.)

Since the 1920s, the southwest corner of Colorado has been promoted as the "mystic southwest" and "holiday land," with advertising touting ruins, hot springs, canyons, and mountains with majestic highways connecting them. This photograph shows the old US Highway 160 that was later relocated and paved to provide a fast motorway between Pagosa Springs and Durango. (Courtesy of US Forest Service, Pagosa District.)

In 1951, Mr. and Mrs. J.F. Mathews owned the Piedra Cabins, Tavern and Liquor Store where the Piedra River meets US Highway 160. Promoted as a base for visiting Chimney Rock, it featured good backcountry horseback riding, hunting, and fishing for tourists. Today, various ranchers and backcountry outfitters live off the land along the Piedra River, utilizing agriculture and wilderness tourism endeavors. (Courtesy of the authors' collection.)

In the olden days, travelers' excursions to Chimney Rock were sometimes reported in the newspapers. The *Durango Democrat* reported in May 1928, "The Oliver Boyd, Harry Sharp and Carl Hayden families motored to Chimney Rock, Sunday, and enjoyed a picnic dinner." (Courtesy of US Forest Service, Pagosa District.)

Similarly, the *Durango Evening Herald* reported in 1921 that "Mr. and Mrs. J. C. Jakway, their son, Walter, and Miss Olga Dillon made the trip to Pagosa Springs yesterday and took in the Chimney Rock ruins. They report a splendid trip and a most interesting time at the ruins but ran out of gas on the way home and were delayed several hours." (Courtesy of Laura Whitt.)

Over the last 120 years, there have been various mining activities in the area surrounding Chimney Rock, the most significant of which is the Chimney Rock Coal Mine. The photograph below shows another historic mine, located just south of today's entrance to the monument, on the west side of Stollsteimer Creek and Highway 151. The commodities mined in this area have included coal, gold, silver, uranium, and even geothermal energy. In the 1910 photograph above, a person is seen looking up amidst a pile of mine tailings. (Above, courtesy of BLM–Anasazi Heritage Center; below, courtesy of the authors' collection.)

Just east of US Highways 160 and 151, the Woman's Civic Club of Pagosa Springs erected this historical marker commemorating Albert Pfeiffer. An Indian scout and Kit Carson aid, he "famously killed a Navajo in a knife duel." This duel is claimed to have won the Pagosa Hot Springs for the Utes. Although much speculation surrounds this event, the monument has stood here since 1955. (Courtesy of the authors' collection.)

Stollsteimer Church sits adjacent to the Southern Ute Reservation and was the former site of early San Juan Basin people. Juan and Florian Gallegos's land adjoins here, and they maintain and care for the church today. They are the descendants of R.R. Gallegos, who assisted archaeologist Jean Jeancon in the 1920s excavations at Chimney Rock. (Courtesy of the authors' collection.)

35

Today, the Southern Ute Reservation borders Chimney Rock National Monument. The tribe partners with other caretakers to protect the sacred area. Cultural interpreters identify Pueblo peoples as the direct descendants of the ancestral villagers who inhabited Chaco Canyon and Chimney Rock (among other sites around the Four Corners). Today, people from various tribes of the Southwest return to visit and perform ceremonial dances at Chimney Rock. In these photographs from 1974, a Southern Ute group is taking a tour of the ruins. (Both, courtesy of US Forest Service, Pagosa District.)

The Southern Ute Youth Camp is located on the Southern Ute Reservation at the northwestern boundary of Chimney Rock National Monument. It has served as campgrounds for various groups over the years, including the 1970 and 1971 University of Colorado at Boulder archaeologists' camp. Today, it is used as a summer culture camp for children. (Courtesy of the authors' collection.)

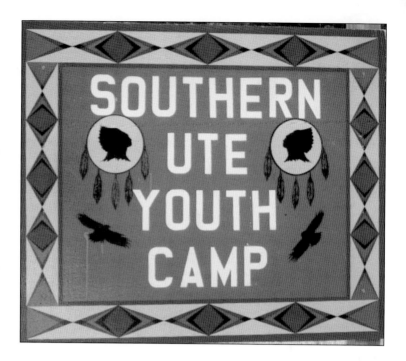

A fascination with the history of the area was not unique to outsiders. In 1924, the Durango chapter of the DAR undertook a program of study of the historical development of the San Juan Basin, including the prehistoric peoples of Chimney Rock. (Courtesy of US Forest Service, Pagosa District.)

The Piedra River and Stollsteimer Creek valleys surrounding Chimney Rock have provided grazing and agricultural fields since the Ancestral Puebloans inhabited the area. In those earlier times, people grew corn, beans, and squash in the valleys and slopes of the area, leaving behind evidence of sophisticated irrigation systems and check dams. In a *Durango Democrat* article from July 27, 1928, the Chimney Rock region's resources are reported as "undeveloped coal deposits, great oil possibilities and a virgin field for the precious minerals prospector. Principle industries of the county are ranching, dairying, cattle and sheep raising, lumber and tie manufacturing." (Above, courtesy of BLM–Anasazi Heritage Center; left, courtesy of the authors' collection.)

In the literary world, fiction authors have found inspiration at Chimney Rock and placed their own creative interpretations within its history. In 2002, James Doss published *White Shell Woman*. Doss used the pinnacles and the Twin Warrior Gods lore as the backdrop for his mystery, which involves a murder, a Ute police detective turned rancher, and the ancient stories and people of the "Ghost Wolf Mesa." In 2006, Sally Crum published a children's story titled *Race to the Moonrise*, which explores the lives of two young traders from prehistoric Mexico and their journey to Chimney Rock. In 2008, Sandi Ault published *Wild Inferno*, a story of conflicts between Southern Utes, white government officials, and a raging forest fire around Chimney Rock and the surrounding lands. These two Sanborn Souvenir Company postcards showcase this literary landmark. (Both, courtesy of the authors' collection.)

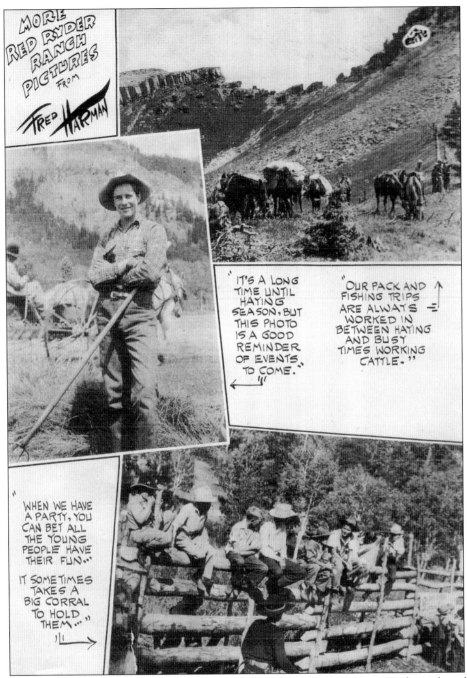

Published in 1946, H.C. Thomas's *Red Ryder and the Adventure at Chimney Rock* was based on the famous newspaper comic strip by Fred Harman. The climax of the story happens when Little Beaver and his bow and arrow rescue Red and two others stranded at the top of Chimney Rock. The son of Red Ryder's creator, Fred Harman III, is seen here as a teenager working on the family's nearby Red Ryder Ranch. Today, he recalls delivering mail on horseback in the late 1930s and early 1940s to Jay Catchpole, a forest ranger up at Chimney Rock's Fire Lookout Tower. (Courtesy of Fred Harman III.)

Three

THE DIGGERS
ARCHAEOLOGISTS MAKE THEIR MARK

The pinnacles have witnessed the excitement of early residents and the erratic interests of the people that followed. After a bustling group of Chacoans and locals made Chimney Rock their home for over 200 years, they disappeared suddenly from the archaeological record, leaving one to speculate about the cause of their exodus. After abandonment, the site languished, becoming overgrown with vegetation and debris, and interest in Chimney Rock's significance waned.

In 1921, Jean Jeancon and crew undertook an archaeological expedition of the Piedra District, supported by the Colorado State Historical and Natural History Society and the University of Denver. Jeancon had been an assistant of Jesse Walter Fewkes while at the Smithsonian Institution's Bureau of Ethnology from 1919 to 1921. His crew's finds ignited scientific interest in Chimney Rock, and the young science of anthropology spread like wildfire in the region. Their records tell a fascinating narrative.

Early archaeologists' observations and discoveries in the 1920s inspired new interest. Jeancon was assisted by a handful of Denverites and locals, including Etienne Renaud, Frank Roberts, J.S. Palmer, and ranchers on the Pargin and Harlan properties, among others. These explorations were followed by Frank Eddy and crew in the 1970s, and, most recently, by Stephen Lekson, Brenda Todd, and crew in 2009. Recently, Wendy Sutton, the USFS archaeologist for the San Juan National Forest, investigated the check dams.

The information gleaned over the course of these investigations regarding the tools used, the pottery and plume holders made, the effigies created, and the feather holders personalizes and connects readers to the nature of the human journey through time.

Jean Jeancon reported in 1922, "The attention of the society was first called to the ruins by Mr. F. O. Reed of the American Railway Express Company, who referred the president of the society to Mr. J. S. Palmer, of Farmington, New Mexico, as one who was familiar with the situation." Much correspondence ensued between locals W.E. Colton and W. Zabriskie and Jeancon, state curator of archaeology and ethnology. Jeancon came to investigate the ruins in April 1921. A permit was issued by the Department of Agriculture for summer excavations. Although locals had known of the ruins surrounding the region for years, this became the first official archaeological investigation. On Saturday June 11, 1921, at 12:30 p.m., a group from the State Historical and Natural History Society and the University of Denver headed south in a loaned, two-ton state highway truck nicknamed "Lizzie." The following two pages are taken from Etienne Renaud's field journal titled "1st Expedition, Summer 1921, Piedra Parada." (Photographs by Etienne Renaud, courtesy of University of Denver Special Collections and Archives.)

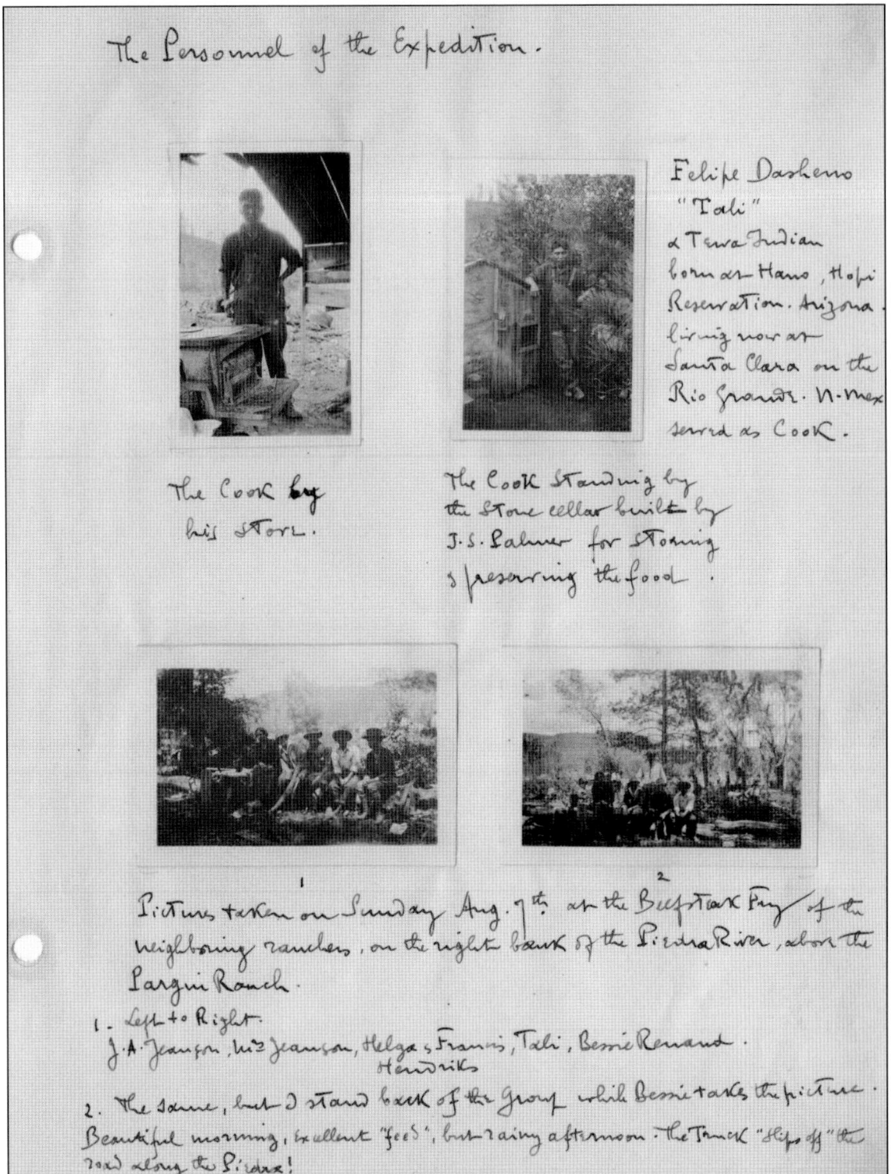
The Personnel of the Expedition.
Felipe Dasheno "Tali" a Tewa Indian born at Hano, Hopi Reservation. Arizona. living now at Santa Clara on the Rio Grande. N-Mex served as Cook.
The Cook by his stove.
The Cook standing by the stone cellar built by J.S. Palmer for storing & preserving the food.
1
2
Pictures taken on Sunday Aug. 7th at the Beefsteak Fry of the neighboring ranchers, on the right bank of the Piedra River, above the Pargin Ranch.
1. Left to Right. J.A. Jeançon, Mrs Jeançon, Helga & Francis, Tali, Bessie Renaud.
Hendriks
2. The same, but I stand back of the group while Bessie takes the picture. Beautiful morning, excellent "feed", but rainy afternoon. The Truck "slips off" the road along the Piedra!

The eight intrepid travelers made their way from Denver to Chimney Rock. They included Jean Jeancon, five University of Denver student archaeologists—George Allan, Leland Anderson, Theodore Concevitch, Charles Earl Mitton, and Frank Roberts—University of Denver romance language professor Etienne Renaud, and Pat Boyle. Amateur archaeologist J.S. Palmer initially guided them up to the ruins. He was a former assistant to Earl Morris at the Aztec Ruins and served as their "stone mason and reconstruction expert." According to field journals and regional newspapers, locals that supported the excavation, scouting, and survey work included W.E. Colton, R.R. Gallegos, Mr. and Mrs. A.J. Nossaman, J.S. Palmer, Floyd Porter, and Pargin and Harlan family members. The cook, Felipe "Tali" Dasheno, was a Tewa Indian (born at Hano, Hopi Reservation in Arizona). At the time, Tali lived at Santa Clara Pueblo on the Rio Grande in New Mexico. (Photographs by Etienne Renaud, courtesy of University of Denver Special Collections and Archives.)

The camps of the 1921 and 1922 archaeology crew flew their "Bone Diggers Union" white flag that had a skull and crossbones on it. The camp was complete with cook shack, cook, wives, and locals from the Pargin and Harlan ranches, as well area residents. The two photographs on this page were taken of their field camp, which was set up just south of Devil Creek. (Courtesy of US Forest Service, Pagosa District.)

Members of the 1920s crews guided and interpreted the Chimney Rock structures for interested visitors. Jean Jeancon claims to have shown more than 500 curious locals around the digs in 1921 alone. Based on the small population of this remote region at the time and the number of tourists willing to partake in the challenging journey, it is uncertain if this number is accurate. (Courtesy of US Forest Service, Pagosa District.)

Jeancon, referred to in field notes as "The Boss," was known to always have his corncob pipe in his mouth while working. After working with Jeancon on excavations at the Chimney Rock ruins during the summers of 1921 and 1923, Frank Roberts took over direction of the expeditions in 1928. Here, his 1920s Ford Model T is parked adjacent to the Great House. (Courtesy of US Forest Service, Pagosa District.)

Frank Roberts (left) and an unidentified man are seen sitting inside one of the excavation sites in 1923. In the early days of the archaeology field, the process of uncovering a site meant that it was essentially destroyed. Photographs were an essential part of the information obtained. (Courtesy of US Forest Service, Pagosa District.)

Frank Roberts stands inside of the Great House East Kiva in 1932. During initial surveying, Jean Jeancon noted this building to be a true circle. At the time, the walls still had exposed original mud plaster in one area. Based on the initial summer of excavations in 1921, Jeancon suspected a connection with the builders and inhabitants of Chaco Canyon's Pueblo Bonito and Aztec Ruins. (Courtesy of BLM–Anasazi Heritage Center.)

Over the years, archaeologists have used various assistants to perform aspects of the excavation process. In September 1925, the *Durango Democrat* reported that 15 prisoners from the Cañon City penitentiary were employed in the Chimney Rock excavations under supervision of the state museum authorities. This 1923 photograph shows Roberts (right) and an unidentified man digging out the Great House East Kiva. (Courtesy of US Forest Service, Pagosa District.)

Chimney Rock   ('67)   7:5 DAB
Larger kiva-state of repair of pueblo
ruin, Chim. Rock--looking approx. N-
C. Breternitz,R.Lister, M. Prince

Between the 1920s and the 1970s, no preservation work took place. Although access is difficult, the sites' open exposure allowed weather and pothunters to wreck havoc. Much architectural integrity was lost. Since 1906, the Antiquities Act has protected these sites and the objects within them. However, the importance of management and preservation of this nonrenewable cultural resource cannot be overstated. In this 1967 photograph, from left to right, Cory Breternitz, Robert Lister, and a Forest Service ranger named Prince survey the state of disrepair above the Great House East Kiva, which is 13 meters in diameter. *Kiva* is a Hopi word for ceremonial house. A large round structure over 10 meters in diameter serving an entire community is known as a Great Kiva. (Photograph by David Breternitz, courtesy of BLM–Anasazi Heritage Center.)

When archaeological work was being done at Chimney Rock in years past, the crews would set up tent camps down along Devil Creek at the Southern Ute Youth Camp by permission of the tribe. Because the crew was also doing survey work for the tribe at the time, permission was granted for a fee. (Courtesy of BLM–Anasazi Heritage Center.)

In 1972, the Yellowjacket USFS Ranger Station served as the archaeologists' campground for the University of Colorado at Boulder crew. The ranger station was located just another mile west along US Highway 160, and it provided running water, bathrooms, and telephones for the crew. Here, Alan Simmons is seen in front of the station. (Photograph by David Breternitz, courtesy of Cory Breternitz.)

In 1977, Frank Eddy wrote, "Since there is no sign of warfare, trade, or other practical reason why the occupants of the Chimney Rock Pueblo should construct their home 1,000 feet above the canyon floor, a religious motivation to build and live up near the gods seems to be the most compelling motive for what was otherwise a difficult living arrangement." The remote location of the mesa also makes for difficult access for archaeology crews needing supplies, especially water. In the above 1970 photograph, trucks are pulling the water truck up to the mesa top for work and crew needs. (Both, photograph by David Breternitz, courtesy of Cory Breternitz.)

The world of Southwestern archaeology is comprised of a tight-knit group of colleagues. From the late 1800s to the present day, there are a handful of archaeologists that have dug, stabilized, or managed various districts. In this 1970 photograph, Robert Lister (left) and Al Lancaster, two such archaeologists, are gathered at site 5AA92. (Photograph by David Breternitz, courtesy of Cory Breternitz.)

Frank Eddy began his archaeology career at Point of Pines field school, where many Southwest archaeologists began their careers. He earned his bachelor of arts in 1952 and his master of arts in anthropology in 1958. He was the curator of the Laboratory of Anthropology at the Museum of New Mexico in Santa Fe. He directed a crew from the University of Colorado, working at Chimney Rock from 1970 to 1972. (Photograph by David Breternitz, courtesy of Cory Breternitz.)

Various organizations have provided resources to support the preservation work at Chimney Rock National Monument. According to the Colorado Office of Archaeology and Historic Preservation, the State Historical Fund has provided over $100,000 in grants for survey and interpretation work at the site. Here, a group of archaeologists gather to begin a day's work in the summer of 1971. (Photograph by David Breternitz, courtesy of Cory Breternitz.)

Many present-day archaeologists are the children of senior archaeologists and were raised in the field. In this photograph, Cory Breternitz is shown uncovering Chimney Rock's site 5AA92 while in his teens. He has gone on to create his own career in archaeology. He is the son of David Breternitz, a prominent Southwestern archaeologist noted for directing the University of Colorado Mesa Verde Research Center and the Dolores Project. (Courtesy of BLM–Anasazi Heritage Center.)

Archaeologists have historically been called diggers or shovelbums, and it is no secret why. With a shovel in hand, the work of digging and displacing dirt can last for many weeks during a summer excavation. Archaeologists have been surveying and digging up stone, bone, clay, and fiber in the Southwest since the 19th century. Discovered artifacts have provided invaluable information to the study and understanding of cultures both past and present. Changing values and new legislation have dramatically changed the practices and use of found objects over the years. (Both, courtesy of BLM–Anasazi Heritage Center.)

Modern machines assist with the excavating efforts. However, the bulk of the work has always involved extensive, careful, manual labor using hand tools and sweat. Challenges of the seasonal work include interaction with wildlife—bugs, snakes, bears, and mountain lions—as well as the constant thirst and hunger of crewmen suffering through extreme temperatures and weather. (Courtesy of BLM–Anasazi Heritage Center.)

Being on an archaeological dig is not all pick-and-shovel work. Earl Morris once noted that a crewman needed "sufficient mental alertness quickly to recognize the object which his pick point or shovel blade has laid bare." Here, Kelly Masterson (right) and Alan Simmons work at the Pit House site in the 1970s. (Courtesy of BLM–Anasazi Heritage Center.)

A major element of archaeological work is the recording and documenting of data through notes, illustrations, and photographs of the area before, during, and after the excavations have taken place. Accurate and precise documentation provides a repository of information that can be used for years after the site work is completed. In this 1969 photograph, a member of the crew diligently records everything of significance. (Courtesy of BLM–Anasazi Heritage Center.)

The archaeological endeavor presents many perplexing questions about the past and the future, and the field is driven by this inquiry. With his feet placed firmly on the ground, there is something very compelling about the way this unidentified man is seen sitting above a site in 1969. (Courtesy of BLM–Anasazi Heritage Center.)

In this 1969 photograph, a crewman is seen recording data about site 5AA17, adjacent to Stollsteimer Church. The church still stands today—situated along the Piedra River and US Highway 151—and is the location of annual celebrations of the Feast of St. Francis. (Courtesy of BLM–Anasazi Heritage Center.)

Empty space does not necessarily mean without evidence of use or meaning. The trained eye uses clues of geography, geology, materials placement, soil, and clearing pattern to identify possible artifacts or ruins. In this 1970 image, Vito Valez, a visiting Honduran government archaeologist, sits near outlying site 5AA100. (Courtesy of BLM–Anasazi Heritage Center.)

Taken from atop the Great House's East Kiva, this July 1971 photograph allows readers to peek into the Great House West Kiva and the busy work of rebuilding a ruin wall. Frank Eddy is seen here discussing the work with Jack Fitzgerald. (Courtesy of BLM–Anasazi Heritage Center.)

Chimney Rock has always had the remarkable ability to elicit awe and wonder from people. One senses the early visitors' energy and former presence, and is struck by appreciation and curiosity about the ways their lives unfolded. Here, Barbara Breternitz and Jim Otis ready for the West Kiva stabilization in 1971. (Photograph by David Breternitz, courtesy of Cory Breternitz.)

In this view looking north in 1967, crewman Cory Breternitz is dwarfed by the 54-inch-wide Great House north wall that he is standing atop. Noting the buttresses to his right, a crewman would have witnessed these thousand-year-old structures in a state of disrepair after years of exposure to weather, human, and animal activity. These walls evidence skill and care in their construction. Engineering abilities are evident and the labor is tangible. A Great House, as known in Chacoan cultural sites, was core-and-veneer sandstone masonry, perhaps multistory, with high-ceilinged rooms, and incorporated dual kivas. Florence Lister writes that it was unlike any other architectural complex on the Piedra River. There is a similar great house, on the nearby Peterson Mesa, identified as the C-block structure. (Courtesy of BLM–Anasazi Heritage Center.)

The practice of using masons and crewmen from the Navajo Nation has taken place for the last 100 years in archaeological work throughout the Southwest, including Mesa Verde National Park. Renowned for their training and skills in archaeological reconstruction, Navajo masons were recruited for the work of stabilizing the structures at Chimney Rock several times throughout the last 40 years. Their lineage may have provided an understanding of the best designs and materials for these walls, due to their interactions with Pueblo peoples in the Gobernador area. These "pueblitos" (small villages) were multiroom masonry dwellings built on mesa tops, and they had to withstand severe weather—not unlike Chimney Rock. (Both, courtesy of US Forest Service, Pagosa District.)

Between the 1920s and the 1970s, no formal excavations took place. During that time, the region had gained enough notoriety that some sites were being vandalized. In the foreground is evidence of a pothunted site. In the background, Chuck Adams and Alan Simmons labor over rocks near the unexcavated pit house structures. (Courtesy of BLM–Anasazi Heritage Center.)

In 1931, Southwestern archaeologist Earl Morris said, "The notion seems rather current that the archaeologist lives about the most thrilling and carefree existence to be found in modern times. [But] those who live by archaeology encounter more difficulties and disappointments, and fully as much hard work, both physical and mental, as fall to the lot of the average mortal." (Courtesy of BLM–Anasazi Heritage Center.)

Earl Morris once said, "Pick and shovel are the tools of a lowly and misunderstood profession . . . There are almost as many different kinds of picks and shovels as there are artists' brushes, and each one is shaped for a definite and specific skill . . . If ever the touch of the master is needed, it is in archaeological excavation." (Courtesy of BLM–Anasazi Heritage Center.)

During archaeological fieldwork, some processes are done on-site, while others must be done back at the lab. At some sites, archaeomagnetic signature remains have been found in materials. In this photograph, Kathy Amy is working on this type of sample testing near the Pit House sites. (Courtesy of BLM–Anasazi Heritage Center.)

Women have played an important role in archaeology since the beginning of the field. Notable female archaeologists who have worked on or with materials from Chimney Rock include Florence Lister, Elizabeth Morris, Sharon Hatch, Marcia Truell Newren, Brenda Todd, and Wendy Sutton. Joan Ricker is seen here enjoying herself during the 1970s excavations. (Courtesy of BLM–Anasazi Heritage Center.)

Although Earl Morris collected wood beam samples for the Tree-Ring Laboratory at the University of Arizona in 1921, Jeancon's crew was famously known for burning wood beams in their campfires during the 1920s. During the 1970s excavations, one of Frank Eddy's goals was to collect and date wood samples. Here, Kelly Masterson inspects a piece of burned wood during those years. (Courtesy of BLM–Anasazi Heritage Center.)

Here, Frank Eddy is looking down from a photography ladder over the Parking Lot site in 1970. The ladder, supported by wires and held in place by rocks at the bottom, affords a vantage point for necessary planning. In addition to his research and excavations at Chimney Rock, Eddy did the archaeological research for the nearby Navajo Reservoir Project in 1961 and has written of its prehistory as well. It is thought that some of the cultures that lived in this location interacted with the Chacoans in the development of the Chimney Rock construction. Eddy's suggestion that this was a perfect place to observe the stars ignited John McKim Malville's interest and the subsequent documentation work that led to it being confirmed as a place where a major lunar standstill is observed between the pinnacles every 18.6 years. (Courtesy of BLM–Anasazi Heritage Center.)

Stephen Lekson (left) has spent 30 years studying the history and significance of the ancient Southwest. Today, he is the curator of anthropology at the Museum of Natural History at the University of Colorado. During the summer of 2009 (after three years of stabilization planning), he led a team from the University of Colorado at Boulder at Chimney Rock. It performed fill reduction and excavation, architectural documentation, and structural work on the Great House Pueblo. Excavations were done on Rooms 5 and 7, where the fill was reduced by 60 centimeters in each room in order to better stabilize the walls. One-quarter of each room was excavated down to the bedrock. Here, Lekson and University of Colorado at Boulder graduate student Brenda Todd (right) oversee the crew. (Courtesy of Stephen Lekson.)

During the 2009 excavations, six students and a director from University of Colorado at Boulder performed fill reduction and archaeological investigations at the Great House. These were the first excavations performed since the 1970s. (Courtesy of Stephen Lekson.)

Shown here, standing at the base of the Chimney Rock Fire Lookout Tower, is the 2009 University of Colorado at Boulder crew. The crew includes, from left to right, Jason Chuipka, Allison Bredthauer, Jakob Sedig, Erin Baxter (in doorway), Brenda Todd, Kellam Throgmorton, and Stephen Lekson. (Photograph by Jim Scott, courtesy of Stephen Lekson.)

Four

EVIDENCE EXPOSED
ARCHAEOLOGICAL SITES
AND ARTIFACTS

Only a handful of the more than 200 archaeological sites that exist at Chimney Rock have been excavated. Pottery discovered was made of local clays and has been found to exhibit degrees of Chacoan influence. Corrugated pots for storage vessels were the most utilized. Piedra black-on-white, Tusayan polychrome, Payan corrugated, and Chacoan pots were also found at these sites.

Two large excavated sites on the High Mesa are designated Great Kivas. The East Kiva is nearly 44 feet across with a bench-like structure, foot drums (stone-lined vaults), and a fire pit (or altar). It has not been determined if this construction had a roof or not.

The Pit House dwellings in the High Mesa area that have been excavated held many treasures. Numerous artifacts have been uncovered and photographed, and nearly all are stored at the Anazasi Heritage Center in Dolores, Colorado. Some of the artifacts recovered and restored include household goods, utilitarian tools, and ceremonial objects. Stone axe heads, anvils, manos, metates, food storage containers, serving ladles, and other kitchen-like utensils have been found. Plume holders found are ceramic and contain four holes for the placement of feathers. More have been found here than elsewhere in the Four Corners. It has been noted that stone basins often indicate a water collection spot nearby, and the one at Chimney Rock exemplifies this due to evidence of a water collection pond near the stone circle.

Archaeoastronomy evidence has authenticated the connection with the Chaco Canyon center and provides moon watchers with significant viewpoints to observe the transit of the moon to the north and back. The Stone Basin located near the Pit House has been noted to be a reference point used in the construction of the Great Wall and a viewing place for the lunar standstill.

Archaeologists are finding new ways to date and explore sites, and it is expected that the research here will continue to evolve and find new clues.

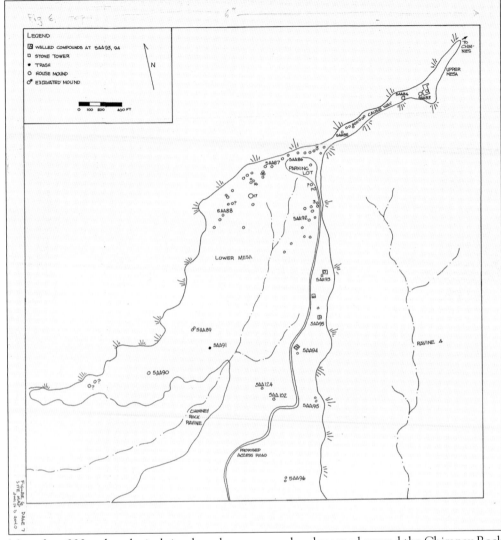

More than 200 archaeological sites have been surveyed and mapped around the Chimney Rock region. It is believed that the region encompasses eight residential village clusters (seven east of the Piedra River and one on top of Peterson Mesa). The sites are marked using the Smithsonian system—for example, 5AA86. The 5 stands for Colorado; AA stands for Archuleta County; and the two-digit number stands for the site number recorded in the state archaeologist's office for that county. Since the time of this illustration, the "proposed access road" has become the main road from the visitor's center below the rim to the top of the cuesta. The most accessible sites at Chimney Rock are (listed by site number and general name) 5AA83, Great House; 5AA84, Guard House; 5AA86, Parking Lot site; and 5AA88, Ravine site (includes the Great Kivas and Pit House). This map represents Chimney Rock's upper mesa group of sites and was compiled by the Division of Engineering Branch of Surveys and Maps in 1969. (Courtesy of US Forest Service, Pagosa District.)

The two photographs on this page were taken from the same point of reference—looking south with the Great House in the foreground. Believed to have been occupied between 1076 and 1125, the Great House compound is estimated by archaeologists to have included at least 35 rooms and two kivas, and was built using 6 million stones. This photograph was taken in September 1941. (Courtesy of US Forest Service, Pagosa District.)

In this 2009 photograph, Huerfano Peak is the farthest point on the horizon and the most prominent feature in the northern Chaco Basin. It is believed that fire beacons signaled a visual communication line—conveying information between Chimney Rock and Chaco Canyon's Pueblo Alto—via this peak. (Courtesy of Stephen Lekson.)

As historic preservationist Frank Matero said, "A ruin, by definition, is something there is less and less of. Sites are not static. They are always in a state of unbecoming." When visiting an archaeological site, what one experiences may shape his relationship to the past. If there has been reconstruction or alterations, a conscious attempt has been made to evoke certain emotions in the visitor. (Courtesy of BLM–Anasazi Heritage Center.)

After a few years of initial work, Jean Jeancon and Frank Roberts moved on to other projects, thus never realizing their dream to create a tourist park that would rival Mesa Verde National Park, established in 1906 and located 85 miles west of Chimney Rock. (Courtesy of US Forest Service, Pagosa District.)

Years of preservation activity have been sporadic due to funding, interest, and management changes. Time, vandals, and natural elements have taken their toll on the ruins. Here, Forest Service ranger Prince, Robert Lister, and Cory Breternitz survey a site's deterioration in 1967. (Photograph by David Breternitz, courtesy of BLM–Anasazi Heritage Center.)

Chimney Rock . ('67)   7:6 DAB
Looking E across smaller kiva to house
mound--pueblo ruin, Chimney Rock--
M. Prince. R. Lister. C. Breternitz

In this July 1971 photograph, Jack Fitzgerald is repairing walls in the Great House Kiva. In this area's excavations, the crew uncovered nine vaults with plank coverings thought to store ceremonial items. This structure is believed to be a locally constructed variant of a Great Kiva because of a short bench with tapered ends and subfloor stone-lined vaults. (Courtesy of BLM–Anasazi Heritage Center.)

The Great House is the most awe-inspiring prehistoric structure in the Chimney Rock National Monument. Theories have evolved regarding the construction of the Great House. It is thought to have been built by local inhabitants to imitate the great structures at Chaco Canyon. However, recent research identifies the construction was performed (or at least supervised) by Chaco masons who had relocated to Chimney Rock, possibly because of its astronomical and spiritual significance. Part of the Great House was two stories and was covered with plaster (now lost due to weathering). This structure followed Jesse Walter Fewkes's original mission from the Smithsonian (at Mesa Verde) to stabilize the site in order to present it to the public. Today, it is certainly the main draw at Chimney Rock National Monument. (Courtesy of BLM–Anasazi Heritage Center.)

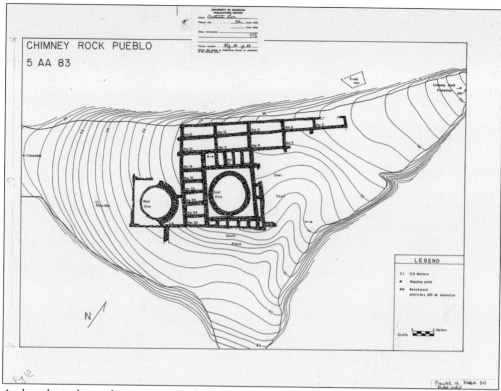

CHIMNEY ROCK PUEBLO
5 AA 83

LEGEND

Archaeological sites that are open to the public require high-quality stabilization work. Conjecture about the early people's lives would not be possible without the meticulous and skilled efforts of the masons. Although techniques and materials have changed over the years, the goal of providing access remains fundamental to these custodians. Today, tourists can walk around various features of the ruins because of the strength of the stabilization efforts. From this 1967 overview photograph, the viewer can see the pueblo in the same plan view as in the illustration above. (Above, courtesy of BLM–Anasazi Heritage Center; below, photograph by Glenn Raby, courtesy of US Forest Service, Pagosa District.)

Chimney Rock structures exhibit Chacoan architectural traits, such as straight walls, square corners, pecked and smoothed stones, chinking, interior wall doorways, and the appearance of a planned design. These photographs exhibit the supposed view that the Great House was built in two different construction phases (believed to be 1076 and 1093). In 1921, Etienne Renaud noted, "The rather artistic effort obtained by placing two or three thin slabs together between rows of big stones. This recalls similar types of masonry as found at Aztec and in the ruins of Chaco Cañon [New Mexico]." (Both, courtesy of US Forest Service, Pagosa District.)

The original masonry walls were covered with adobe plaster in a manner similar to the methods used by modern pueblo masons. Frank Eddy determined that the sandstone and clay adobe were sourced from the slopes of the East Mesa. Because of the core-and-veneer masonry exhibited, interpreters have determined that construction was performed by Chacoan masons and is not simply a superficial imitation of the style of Chaco architecture. The Great House showcases finely chinked core-and-veneer walls with rectangular, brick-like stones flush to the exposed wall. In the early 1970s, they primarily used Portland cement in wall stabilization work. From the late 1970s through the early 1990s, archaeologists performed experimental mortar work, sourcing local adobe clay on some of the walls for stabilization. (Courtesy of BLM–Anasazi Heritage Center.)

The Great House was left open and exposed for 50 years because after the first excavations in 1921, no part of the structure was backfilled. The Great House has no foundation footings or trenches because it is built on solid, sloped, footed bedrock. (Courtesy of BLM–Anasazi Heritage Center.)

This 1971 view of the Great House shows Rooms 31–35, located between the Great House kivas. The wooden roofs of these rooms were laid in a herringbone pattern and supported by the walls. The entrance was from a hatch above. Various rooms were used for different functions, including living rooms, storage, preparing, heating, and cooking food. (Courtesy of BLM–Anasazi Heritage Center.)

The mound site 5AA92 was located on the west side of the access road. Road construction in 1970–1971 severely damaged this site and others, but provided driving access for future visitors who are now able to journey up the mesa to view them. Here, Cory Breternitz excavates the northwest room. (Courtesy of USDA. Forest Service, Pagosa District.)

During the course of excavations, archaeology crews expose, process, and record artifacts and information found at the site. This photograph shows how the mound site 5AA92 appeared when its excavations were complete. The unpaved access road can be seen in the left of the photograph. (Courtesy of BLM–Anasazi Heritage Center.)

Jean Jeancon's crew uncovered the Great House East Kiva in 1921. This ventilation tunnel provided a channel for fresh air to flow through into the kiva. Renaud noted in 1921, "The existence of this 'double ventilator' is a unique fact of a problem still unsolved." Today, it is believed to be evidence of a remodel, during which the floor was raised. (Courtesy of BLM–Anasazi Heritage Center.)

This 1987 photograph shows the ventilation shaft located at Mound Three in the Parking Lot site. The shaft channeled fresh air down into the open room. Although the rooms in this area were round, they contained a fire basin and artifacts used for everyday living, and are thus considered "above ground pit houses" (as David Breternitz called them). (Courtesy of US Forest Service, Pagosa District.)

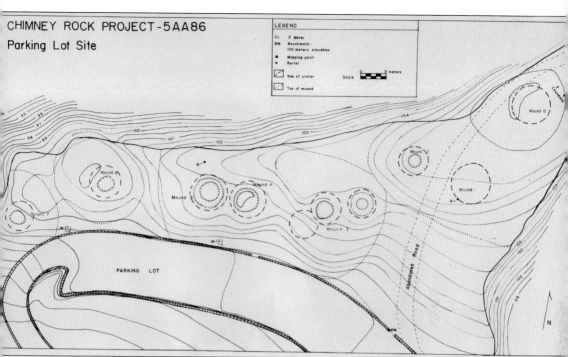

The Parking Lot site, 5AA86, stretches out along a wide swath of land and was originally excavated by Frank Eddy and crew in 1970 and 1971. It is distinct because it is here that archaeologists first identified the wall construction to be a local variant from the Great House construction style. It was determined that these buildings were contemporary to the Great House and were likely made by masons from the area, not by Chaco migrants. Although theories have been developed about the people—through a great deal of study and interpretation—there remains a need to fill in aspects of life when no translatable evidence remains. Those who possess a scientific imagination may utilize both aspects of evidence and (supposed) information in order to recreate plausible answers to questions. (Courtesy of BLM–Anasazi Heritage Center.)

This 1971 photograph was taken from a helicopter and shows the Parking Lot site (right) and crew's equipment (left). There is documentation that this area was utilized for meat processing by the Ancestral Puebloans. Today, the parking lot is paved and the site is easily accessible for tourists to walk around. (Courtesy of BLM–Anasazi Heritage Center.)

This aerial view shows the three rooms excavated at Mound Three of the Parking Lot site. They were especially distinct because they differed from traditional Chaco and Mesa Verde style round rooms in that they did not contain *sipapus* (emergent basins). With other clues, the archaeologists determined that these were not kivas but rather domestic living rooms. (Courtesy of BLM–Anasazi Heritage Center.)

The Ravine site, 5AA88, is one of the most accessible of the excavated sites on the Chimney Rock Mesa. The Great Kiva measuring 12 meters across is adjacent to this site. The excavation, stabilization, and construction of this kiva eventually led to an important stop along the tourist trail. Since the 1980s, it has also served as a place of dance for tribal ceremonies. The structure was originally roofed and contained 14 subfloor vaults, nine of which were covered with lids. This aerial photograph was taken prior to the beginning of the excavations directed by Marcia Truell Newren in the summer of 1972. (Both, courtesy of BLM–Anasazi Heritage Center.)

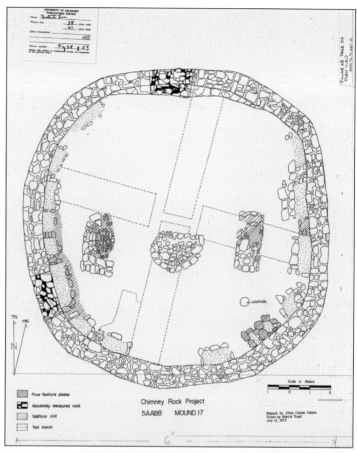

Chimney Rock Project

5AA88   MOUND 17

Unlike many of the other Southwestern ancestral villages, Chimney Rock had no shortage of wood because of the adjacent San Juan forests. Towering pine and spruce caused many early scholars to identify Chimney Rock as the "lumber town" of Chaco. It is not a coincidence that the adjacent town was named Arboles (Spanish for "trees"). These great ponderosa pines have overtaken the prehistoric stone masonry of the Chimney Rock walls. Prior to excavations, crewmen from the US Forest Service came with chain saws to clear these massive tree trunks in order to access the site. This practice is not uncommon in archaeological excavation work when there are forests surrounding structures. (Both, courtesy of BLM–Anasazi Heritage Center.)

The kiva (a Hopi term for underground chamber used for social or ceremonial use) served various purposes depending on the architecture of the structure. With a *sipapu* (emergent hole), the room was regarded as a space for ceremony. The roofs of the kiva structures were used as plazas and provided access into the room. (Courtesy of US Forest Service, Pagosa District.)

Today, curious tourists can explore this pit house group located in the Ravine site. This circular living room has three adjacent storage and milling rooms. Evidence found here includes pottery rings, roof construction, milling bins, and storage subfloor vaults filled with maize. Most exciting were the uncovered sherds of five corrugated jars still containing maize, beans, and wild plant seeds. (Courtesy of BLM–Anasazi Heritage Center.)

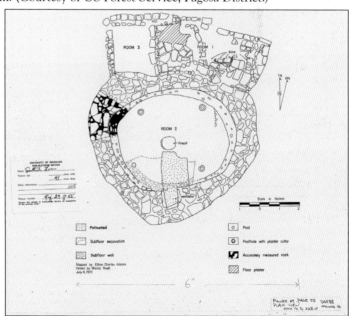

Pottery and other ceramics have a life of creation, use, and returning to the earth. They represent a fine marriage of function and form. This photograph shows fragments recovered during the 1970s from site 5AA84, originally named the Guard House by Jean Jeancon because of its location along the isthmus. (Courtesy of BLM–Anasazi Heritage Center.)

Much of the pottery found at archaeological sites is broken. The restoration of these pots requires great skill and patience. In years past, the restoration work was done in the field before transport to the museum. Today, the work is done under controlled conditions at the lab. This Payan corrugated pot was found in pieces. (Courtesy of BLM–Anasazi Heritage Center.)

Unlike at cliff and cave sites, few baskets have been found around Chimney Rock. Sites in canyons and cliffs do not experience the effects of weather as much as those on mesa tops. Pottery, however, has been plentiful. This Payan corrugated pot was uncovered in the Great House and is housed in the Anasazi Heritage Center collections in Dolores, Colorado. (Courtesy of BLM–Anasazi Heritage Center.)

The Payan corrugated ware was later attributed to the Gallina region of north-central New Mexico, a region occupied before and after Chimney Rock's height of occupancy. It is identified as utility ware rather than ceremonial ware because of its shape and outer texture. (Courtesy of the authors' collection.)

Jean Jeancon recovered this magnificent artifact in 1922 at the Chimney Rock Great House. Referred to as a duck pot, it is 46 centimeters long and is housed in the History Colorado collections. Duck pots are the most common effigy vessels of the Chaco cultural sites, some of which resemble the actual animal more than others. (Courtesy of US Forest Service, Pagosa District.)

Of the pottery uncovered at Chimney Rock's Great House, 10 percent was of the Gallup black-on-white variety from Chaco Canyon. Nearly 60 percent of the pottery was a local variant of Chacoware—created by using crushed Chaco pots for temper. Today, potters and artisans are creating replicas inspired by the early designs of pottery. This is a duckpot replica created by local artist Clink Swink. (Courtesy of the authors' collection.)

This nonutilitarian earthenware was found in Room 8 of the Great House and is identified today as a plume holder. Twelve of the 18 known holders found in Chaco sites were made from Chimney Rock clay. When Frank Roberts first stumbled upon this "curious article of pottery," he noted that it "was possibly used as a plume holder to wear on [the] forehead." (Courtesy of BLM–Anasazi Heritage Center.)

Archaeologists interpret the plume holders both as objects that represent ceremonial activities and as evidence of trade with peoples all over the ancient Southwest. Four were found in Room 2 of the Pit House site, two were found in the Salvage site, and two were found in the Ridge House site. (Courtesy of BLM–Anasazi Heritage Center.)

Throughout Ancestral Puebloan sites, manos (hand stones) and metates (grinding slabs) have been recovered. They were used to grind berries, grain, leaves, nuts, seeds, and stems. This fine example was uncovered near stone-grinding bins in the Ravine site. (Courtesy of BLM–Anasazi Heritage Center.)

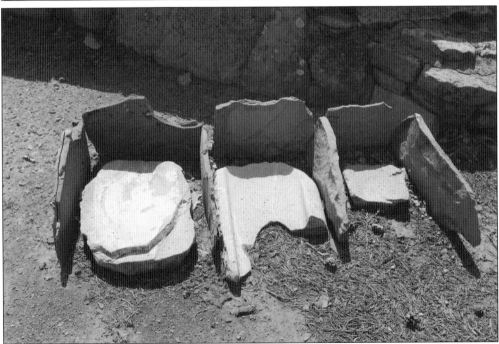

As author and photographer John Ninnemann wrote, "We know that the people who have lived here are in some way still present." There is no better example of this sentiment than stumbling upon a row of milling bins. It is easy to imagine early people bent over the bins, grinding kernels in preparation for the evening's meal. (Courtesy of the authors' collection.)

Corn is one of the Three Sisters crops that were cultivated around the Southwest, both prehistorically and historically. It was one of the most important staples of people's diets in this region. In this 2009 photograph, Allison Bredthauer is excavating a pile of burned corn in the Great House Room 7 during the University of Colorado at Boulder's excavations. (Courtesy of Stephen Lekson.)

Stone artifacts, such as axes, choppers, hammers, scrapers, and round cobbles for mud construction, were plentiful around the region. They had various uses, including hunting and food preparation. This large stone axe head was uncovered from the Parking Lot site in the early 1970s. (Courtesy of BLM–Anasazi Heritage Center.)

Large animals were plentiful around the Piedra River. Many were seasonal migrators, such as mule deer and elk. They provided a vital source of protein, as well as skin, bone, and antlers. This bone fragment was found during the excavations of the Ravine site. (Courtesy of BLM–Anasazi Heritage Center.)

The antlers of deer and elk were used as scraping tools, flaking tools, and stone-pecking tools, as well as awls and fetishes. Oftentimes, the people would harden the antler in the fire. This antler was excavated from the Ravine site in the 1970s. (Courtesy of BLM–Anasazi Heritage Center.)

In an attempt to maximize runoff, residents constructed check dams. These were intended to conserve water and enhance agricultural efforts. In the arid Southwest, subsistence settlement and endeavors are affected by climate and environment. The findings of check dams illustrate the builders' engineering skill within environmental constraints. Here, Lyniss Steinert, a Chimney Rock tour guide, showcases evidence of check dams found along the Lower Mesa. (Courtesy of the authors' collection.)

Stone basins are another element found at Chaco cultural sites. A low stone wall originally surrounded the circular Stone Basin at Chimney Rock. It has been found to align with the sunrise on the summer solstice and the Crab Nebula supernova (seen in 1054), and with the spring and fall equinoxes (in alignment with the Great House several hundred yards north). (Courtesy of US Forest Service, Pagosa District.)

The Chimney and Companion Rock pinnacles are known as a site of archaeoastronomy, or cultural astronomy. Every 18.6 years, the moon rises between these two monoliths, as seen by someone standing at the Great House. This occurs when the moon reaches its northernmost point. It has been recorded (in recent times) in 1988 and 2004, and will next be on display in 2022. (Courtesy of US Forest Service, Pagosa District.)

Wood beam samples from the Great House (foreground) date to 1076 and 1094, thus coinciding with major lunar standstills. Although some of the wood may have been reused, it provides evidence of construction dates. Inhabitants observed the Crab Nebula supernova in 1054, Halley's Comet in 1066, and a total solar eclipse in 1097. This evidence suggests that the monument is a solar and lunar observatory. (Photograph by Helen Richardson, courtesy of US Forest Service, Pagosa District.)

The nearest ridgeline (in the background) is called Peterson Mesa. This is where C-block sites have been found. They were a likely viewing point for inhabitants gazing across the Piedra River to the two pinnacles during the fall and spring equinoxes. Structures there have been noted since 1921, when Etienne Renaud recorded, "Ruins are reported to exist in large number on the mesa seen across the Piedra." (Courtesy US Forest Service, Pagosa District.)

The tumbled structures once occupied by thousands of men, women, and children leave a silent vacancy that inhabits visitors. There is no purely translatable record of the people's songs, stories, or rituals of everyday life. Therefore, archaeologists require a heightened sense of imagination to re-create life among these structures. (Courtesy US Forest Service, Pagosa District.)

The peoples of the Southwest maintain a unique perspective of space and time. The interpretation of life through the ascent and descent into other worlds and the importance of the four cardinal directions are represented in motifs, architecture, and ceremonial evidence around the ancient world. (Courtesy US Forest Service, Pagosa District.)

The complex cosmology of these people tells a story of dualism: sun and moon, mother and father, winter and summer. In one tale, the twin sons of the sun, named differently among regional tribes, ascend to the upper cosmic world to visit their father and to slay monsters of this world. (Courtesy of US Forest Service, Pagosa District.)

Astronomer and astrophysicist John McKim Malville writes about the "astronomer priests of the ancient Southwest" and their knowledge of the cosmos—the evidence of which can be seen at Chimney Rock and other Chaco cultural sites. He is attributed with recording—while standing at the site of the Great House on top of the mesa—Chimney Rock's archaeoastronomical significance by observing and studying the evidence of the major lunar standstill that can be seen rising between the stone pinnacles. He believes that calendrical information (such as the timing of moon- and sunrises on solstices and equinoxes) was recorded by sky watchers and conveyed to other Chaco villages. This information sets dates for ceremonial or economic festivals. He theorized that "prehistoric inhabitants of the area may have been observing moonrise and equinoctial sunrise between the rock spires as early as the eight or ninth century." Helen Richardson took this photograph between 2005 and 2007 during a major lunar standstill event. (Courtesy of US Forest Service, Pagosa District.)

Each month during the summer open season at Chimney Rock National Monument, a group of volunteers hosts a full moon program atop the Upper Mesa. Speakers share legends and scientific research related to the spires and the culture of the early people. They explain that early sky watchers were known to have a strong relationship with the sun, moon, and stars. In this photograph, visitors today enjoy a full moonrise over the mountains to the east. During these events, a conscious attempt is made to evoke emotions and provide a visceral experience for visitors. They are often serenaded by flute music and told interpretations of native folklore. This type of experience is what early archaeologists have been trying to provide for visitors, in different ways, for nearly 150 years. (Courtesy of Maia Banks.)

It is not hard to see how the pinnacles of Chimney Rock are recognized by Southwest elders as the Twin Warrior Gods made manifest into stone. Tribal lore from Navajo and various pueblos of the Southwest references these gods as major deities. In Navajo mythology, the War Twins are named Monster Slayer and Born-for-Water. Their father is the Sun and their mother is the Moon (or White Shell Woman). The twins are represented in the sky by the morning and the evening stars. Pictographs of these gods were found beside the San Juan River within a few miles of the site. This region is now submerged under the Navajo Reservoir. Other Southwest rock art of the twins shows them as symbols (two parallel lines) or as anthropomorphs with red hands, ponytails, and bows. This photograph was taken looking northwest from Stollsteimer Mesa in October 1944. (Courtesy of US Forest Service, Pagosa District.)

Origin myths of underworld migrations and the worship of sun, moon, and rain spirits are prevalent in legends, shrines, and etched symbols throughout the Southwest. In the 1960s, ethnographic accounts recorded by Florence Hawley Ellis identified the Chimney Rock shrine that was used by the Day People of the Taos Pueblo. Dr. Alfonso Ortiz, a cultural anthropologist and tribal member from San Juan, New Mexico, recorded an elder's narrative that mapped Chimney Rock's location accurately. In it, the Tewa elder visited the monoliths and, upon approaching them, referred to it as Fire Mountain. "It is just as the old people spoke of it!" the gentleman exclaimed. Ortiz recalls, "As my friend spoke of that remembered place, we realized that we were retracing part of the ancient journey of our people, a journey which began beneath a lake somewhere in this corner of Colorado." (Courtesy of BLM–Anasazi Heritage Center.)

Five

DEDICATED STEWARDS
VOLUNTEERS AND THE FOREST SERVICE

One of the most heartening and inspiring aspects of any preservation effort is the story of the dedicated and passionate stewards. The story of Chimney Rock is no exception. Although found within a geographically remote area, it is remarkable how many people have shown a steadfast dedication to protecting and promoting this monument.

Since the 1970s, groups of volunteers have led tours, written grants, and sought to preserve, protect, and educate the public about the Chimney Rock resources. Original members focused their efforts on protecting the sites from pothunters. They now provide site maintenance, land stewardship projects, interpretive tours, night sky programs, scholarly research, archaeology, and school support—in equal measure. In 2004, the Chimney Rock Interpretive Association (CRIA) became a formal nonprofit organization. Today, it is thriving and has over a hundred members.

In partnership with CRIA, the employees of the US Forest Service, of the San Juan National Forest, Pagosa Ranger District, manage the area's land and resources. Over the years, employees and volunteers—archaeologists, forest rangers, geologists, land managers, and others—have been important players in the care of Chimney Rock. Some of their projects have included site stabilization, wildflower tours, prescribed burns, and the meticulous mapping and recording of over 200 archaeological sites. They continue to manage the land and resources for tribal and public access. With the recent transition to national monument designation, long-term plans continue to shift energies as funds and interests allow.

Due to the cooperative efforts of these dedicated people, Chimney Rock National Monument now protects over six square miles (4,726 acres) in Archuleta County, Colorado.

NOTICE

Ancient ruins, artifacts, fossils and historical remains
are fragile and irreplaceable.

HELP PRESERVE
YOUR AMERICAN HERITAGE

Any person who, without an official permit, injures, destroys,
excavates or removes any historic or prehistoric ruin,
artifact or object of antiquity on the public lands of the
United States is subject to arrest and penalty of law.

Please report all antiquities you find, and any suspected
violations you observe, to the nearest office of the
U.S. Forest Service.

United States Department of Agriculture—Forest Service

According to the National Park Service, "The Antiquities Act [of 1906] is the first law to establish that archaeological sites on public lands are important public resources. It obligates federal agencies that manage the public lands to preserve for present and future generations the historic, scientific, commemorative, and cultural values of the archaeological and historic sites and structures on these lands." Signed into law on June 8, 1906, by Pres. Theodore Roosevelt, the Antiquities Act limited hunting, grazing, and mining, and provided punishment for anyone caught looting or damaging resources. It also defined who was permitted to excavate and conduct research on these lands. Shown here, a historic US Forest Service sign addresses these notions of ownership and control of found objects. This sign includes an image of Chimney Rock National Monument (top right) and Mesa Verde National Park (bottom left). (Courtesy of US Forest Service, Pagosa District.)

PROPERTY BOUNDARY

National Forest land behind this sign

54-2

Custodians of regions endure the challenges of defining who owns the past and who controls the land. They also secure funding to protect the region's resources. The structures at Chimney Rock have been a part of a comparable history of land rights, management, and use negotiations since the first professionals started digging. Similarly, the archaeological remains found therein mean different things to different entities. Local residents, tribes, and government officials all view the assets in their own ways. An incorporation of all of these interests is what drives the current initiatives at Chimney Rock. A July 1928 *Pagosa Springs News* article reports, "The fine collection of relics from Chimney Rock . . . which have been housed in the town library, will be displayed in the new courthouse when completed. The collection is owned by the town of Pagosa, bought by citizens a few years back." (Courtesy of US Forest Service, Pagosa District.)

The forest rangers were required to have "better than average intelligence as they are required to be able to figure stumpage, be familiar with the cattle, horse and sheep business in order to estimate pasturage, meet almost any emergency, mental and physical. They are a clean, manly set of fellows as one would naturally expect . . . They know where the red fox, the marten, lynx, mountain lion, skunk, coyote, bear and deer may be found." This US Forest Service fire lookout tower was constructed (1939–1940) on the top of the Chimney Rock Mesa and in use until 1956. Both rangers and trained lookouts managed the tower. It is also important to note that, in the early days, many women were in charge of the Chimney Rock Fire Lookout Tower. (Both, courtesy of US Forest Service, Pagosa District.)

Fire has always been an integral component of the landscape in the Chimney Rock region. By August of the 1940 fire season, 40 fires—mostly from lightning strikes—had been reported in the area that year. Although these rangers were isolated, locals would periodically bring mail by horseback up to the tower. The ranger or trained lookout kept in contact with the ranger headquarters on a shortwave radio. These 1944 photographs show Ranger Sevilla Martinez watching over the Piedra River valley from the platform. (Both, courtesy of US Forest Service, Pagosa District.)

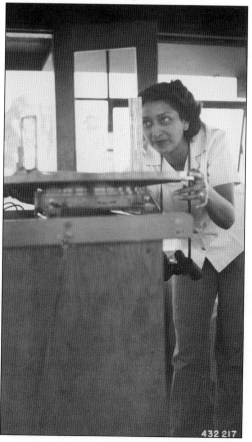

A fire lookout tower is intended to overlook a vast area of forest. During the 1948 summer fire season, Maud Darnell was the fire observer at the lookout. Various friends, including Jean and Joan Bastian, visited her. In 1949, Mrs. Harry Beach was in charge at the tower and her husband would sometimes visit. Many children and spouses of the rangers spent the summer season up at the mesa camping and exploring. The first US Forest Service fire lookout tower was abandoned in 1956. The second was rebuilt in 1987, as seen in this photograph. (Courtesy of US Forest Service, Pagosa District.)

One of the noticeable hazards of being on top of the mesa is the vulnerability to amazing climatic movements. On both of the fire towers, a lightning rod served to protect people caught there during lightning storms. Today, managers of Chimney Rock National Monument make an evacuation call when dangerous weather moves over the mesa. (Courtesy of Mark Roper.)

This fire tower served multiple purposes, including use for occasional fire detection and forest monitoring. Because it provided a 360-degree view, it also served as a stop along the guided interpretive tours and as a viewing platform during special events—major lunar standstills and full moon programs. Here, forest ranger Mark Roper stands on the fire tower platform. (Courtesy of Mark Roper.)

Because the US Forest Service no longer found the fire lookout to be effective—due to lack of visibility of the northern forests, which were blocked by the pinnacles—a ranger was forced to traverse the saddle to the North Mesa. In 2010, the Chimney Rock Fire Lookout Tower was removed using funds from the American Recovery and Reinvestment Act. There were some locals who felt that the tower was still useful for observing forest fires, while others maintained an emotional connection to its presence. Though its removal was necessary to improve the view, there was still a sense of loss felt by some. (Both, courtesy of US Forest Service, Pagosa District.)

As the tower was removed, the panorama of the sky improved dramatically. It was then possible to view the major lunar standstills between the monoliths from the Great House, as people did a thousand years ago. (Courtesy of US Forest Service, Pagosa District.)

As the modern fire tower was removed, the structure of the earlier tower was revealed. The column in the center was built in the 1970s and was not accessible. It merely served as a support for the viewing platforms of both of the towers. (Courtesy of US Forest Service, Pagosa District.)

The Chimney Rock region is situated on the edge of the ponderosa pine and piñon-juniper landscape. Historically, the natural cycle of fires in the region occurred on a 10-to-15-year cycle (ignited most often during the summer monsoon season). These low-intensity ground fires would clean up small fuels. Recently, because of the pine beetle infestation, volatile timber has become more widespread. Homes are often threatened because of certain environmental circumstances that are increasing fire dangers in this area. Firefighters are an important resource for this area and take pride in their abilities and skills in fighting forest fires. In 1878, the poem "Ode to Our Firemen" was penned: "But sound aloud the praises, and give the victor crown / To our noble-hearted Firemen, who fear not danger's frown." (Courtesy of Brandon Oberhardt.)

Today, the US Forest Service is returning to methods of fuel load reduction and natural fire management that have been practiced by cultures all over the world for millennia. The Forest Service creates periodic prescribed burns. They protect Chimney Rock by reducing fuel and protecting the nonrenewable cultural resources that define it. The most recent prescribed burn was completed around the base of the mesa in 2012. Between the hazards of natural events and human error, monitoring by the Forest Service is a necessary and welcome service. (Above, courtesy of the authors' collection; right, courtesy of Brandon Oberhardt.)

It is no coincidence that Chimney Rock is also known as Fire Mountain. Fire has been a vital element of life on this natural, vertical watchtower. It was utilized for sending messages, cooking, making pottery, clearing land to build upon, and heating in the winter. Any of the negative aspects were mitigated by its positive resource. Even the negative features of fire are of benefit to the next generation of activity. Plants and animals adapt to the constraints fire causes, and they welcome the new growth that emerges after a fire. Cabezon Canyon is located just across the highway and southeast of the Chimney Rock National Monument. It has burned several times in recent history, including in 2013. A downed power line started a fire in Cabezon Canyon in 2012. This photograph captures the smoke-filled distance during the September 1987 Cabezon Canyon fire. (Courtesy of US Forest Service, Pagosa District.)

One of the things that surprises visitors as they walk around the Chimney Rock National Monument is that the oldest trees today are only 400 years old. That means that the sites are 600 years older than the trees living here now. US Forest Service chain saw operators were contracted (during the 1970s and later) to remove the large trees that restricted archaeologists' access to sites. This is a noticeable reminder of how nature can obscure evidence of the past with subtlety and power. It requires visitors to imagine a landscape that is different from the prehistoric terrain. (Both, courtesy of US Forest Service, Pagosa District.)

In 1922, archaeologist Jean Jeancon remarked, "The immense amount of labor involved in getting out and preparing the small stones used is startling at best." The extent of the labor involved encompassed the preparation of the stones, the construction, and the maintenance of these exposed structures. Below, these Boy Scouts know firsthand the labor involved in maintaining and rebuilding these structures under the extreme weather conditions at the Chimney Rock Mesa. In these August 1983 photographs, under the sweltering heat, they stabilize the walkway and walls surrounding the Parking Lot sites. (Both, courtesy of US Forest Service, Pagosa District.)

During the 1970s and 1980s, various volunteer efforts were used to maintain and stabilize the structures. In 1983, the Boy Scouts of America helped repair the broken toilet vault located in the parking lot on the Chimney Rock Mesa. Compatible (often local) materials were used for stabilization and presentation of these sites, including soil and stone. Just as modern visitors witness the deconstruction and reconstruction of the walls of these ancient structures, so too will future generations. Time will continue to be a marker that is visible in the stone. (Both, courtesy of US Forest Service, Pagosa District.)

In this early photograph, a bulldozer carves out one of the first roads leading up to the mesa. Coloradoans have a long history of road building through steep terrain. One of the most famous early pathfinders and road builders of this region was Otto Mears. Chimney and Companion Rocks can be seen in the background. (Courtesy of US Forest Service, Pagosa District.)

In 1970, more road-stabilization efforts provided fill to stabilize the dirt road leading to Chimney Rock's mesa top. Today, the windy neck of the road still challenges some vehicles driving on the loose gravel to the parking lot. (Courtesy of US Forest Service, Pagosa District.)

Because of the lacuna between initial excavations and stabilization, there is a separation of time and space and of creation and destruction. Writer Craig Childs remarked after visiting Chimney Rock that the structures have been "beaten into ruins by weather." Skilled masons have been contracted to do the structural repair work using tried-and-true archaeology stabilization techniques. The wattle and daub technique has been used for centuries for building adobe structures and providing mortar. Attention to detail is both required and evident in the recent repairs done in the stabilization work of these sites. (Both, courtesy of US Forest Service, Pagosa District.)

Modern visitors understand archaeological sites and their authenticity through the physical manifestation of their preservation. Sites are recreated into living places through this process (not simply found and frozen in time, as one might believe). The preservation technique of backfilling a site secures its current state for future investigations by reducing the effects of weather and vandalism. However, it removes the present visitor experience. As seen in these photographs, wall stabilization and structure reconstruction recreate a moment in time. It is through the excavation and reconstruction of these structures that the archaeology takes place. (Both, courtesy of US Forest Service, Pagosa District.)

Stabilization work required hauling tons of materials to the sites in buckets with the help of horses, cars, and helicopters. Visitors today are able to walk around (and on top of) the walls because of backbreaking efforts over the last 50 years. (Courtesy US Forest Service, Pagosa District.)

Backfilling a feature or site is done once archaeologists believe they have removed all of the information from the location. It can include stabilizing features (like walls and floors) from undergoing further damage. In this recent photograph, a helicopter is seen dropping backfill for a crew that is working on a feature of the Great House. (Courtesy of US Forest Service, Pagosa District.)

In this 1941 photograph, a forest ranger looks over the deterioration of the Great House ruins. This image is illustrative of what archaeologists encounter in sites after years of open exposure. Other regional archaeological sites that are nested in canyons, caves, and cliffs do not have the same deterioration processes. (Courtesy of US Forest Service, Pagosa District.)

Today, an overhanging shelf built by modern archaeologists protects a portion of the east wall of the Great House. It exhibits the original core-and-veneer architectural style and allows visitors to visually contrast the original architecture (under shelf) with the reconstructed efforts (surrounding wall and buttresses). (Courtesy of the authors' collection.)

From 1968 to 1972, work by various groups, including Youth Corps and the Pagosa Springs Boy Scouts of America Troop 210, has helped construct the access road, parking lot, retaining walls, and trails. In this 1984 photograph, a group of Boy Scouts tours the Great House after completing work. (Courtesy of US Forest Service, Pagosa District.)

Many preservationists believe that the best way to see an archaeological site is to walk on the walls and to take in the plan view. Here, a group tour stands over the Great House East Kiva in the summer season of 1974. (Courtesy of US Forest Service, Pagosa District.)

When negotiations were underway for the mining of coal near Chimney Rock, representatives discussed the impact these activities would have upon the cultural resources. This July 1984 photograph shows a group taking a tour with people from the Colorado Historic Preservation Office and the Colorado Department of Natural Resources. (Courtesy of US Forest Service, Pagosa District.)

The Colorado Archaeological Society was founded in 1935 as an amateur archaeologists group for educating the public and raising awareness about archaeology. Members take tours, attend lectures, and volunteer at regional sites. This October 1982 photograph shows members on a group tour. (Photograph by Robert York, courtesy of US Forest Service, Pagosa District.)

US Forest Service employee Sally Zwisler and a volunteer discuss the structure of one of the Great House rooms. At the beginning of each tourist season, experts lecture at gatherings of the Chimney Rock Interpretive Association. Educational events cover historical and cultural interpretations and hands-on activities like grinding corn, throwing an atlatl, and coiling pots. (Courtesy of US Forest Service, Pagosa District.)

In this May 1986 photograph, a volunteer from the Chimney Rock Archaeological Group gives a tour to a sizable group. In years past, groups numbered more than 50 at one time. Today, guided tour groups are capped at 25 people and are provided several times a day. (Courtesy of US Forest Service, Pagosa District.)

During a 1989 tour, a guide asks visitors to acclimate to the altitude by grabbing a rest on the Stone Sofa. Perched halfway along the cuesta, this landmark provides visitors a perfect southern vista while they listen to information shared by an informed tour guide. (Courtesy of US Forest Service, Pagosa District.)

Members of the Audubon Society visited Chimney Rock Archaeological Area in May 1982. Due to nearly 70 years of peregrine falcon nesting, birders flock to the ruins and pinnacles with their binoculars. (Photograph by Robert York, courtesy of US Forest Service, Pagosa District.)

Here, visitors look south toward Huerfano Peak while veteran tour guide Lyniss Steinert explains how fires were used to communicate with Chaco Canyon across this great distance. In 1996, high school science student Kathryn Freeman tested the communication theory using mirrors to visually communicate with her mother at Huerfano Peak. Her results are now referred to in scientific literature. (Courtesy of the authors' collection.)

Large group events sometimes take place at the Great House. When organizations first charged for special events, the funds were donated to the Hopi Education Fund. This group is gathered to watch the full moon rise while listening to the flute music of Charles Martinez. (Courtesy of Maia Banks.)

Chimney Rock has been stewarded by a long succession of volunteer groups that have performed preservation, education, and tours to visitors. Some of the organized groups are listed chronologically as follows: the Friends of Chimney Rock, formed by a Pagosa Springs volunteer; the Chimney Rock Archaeological Group, formed by Bayfield volunteer Robert Brooks; the San Juan National Forest Association, an official USFS volunteer partner; and Pagosa Chapter of the San Juan Mountains Association, successor to the San Juan National Forest Association. These groups of dedicated custodians have fostered the current state of awareness and preservation. The Chimney Rock National Monument would not exist without their long years of volunteer stewardship. Here, a volunteer opens the summer touring season on May 14, 1993. This visitor's cabin has since burned down. (Courtesy of US Forest Service, Pagosa District.)

Today, the primary stewardship is through a cooperative partnership between the US Forest Service and nonprofit Chimney Rock Interpretive Association (CRIA). This photographs shows visitor Agnes Bell standing in front of Raby Cabin, the welcome center named after longtime custodian Glenn Raby. The cabin is situated at the entrance to the monument. It serves as a museum, bookstore, and check-in point for all visitors during the open season. The open season of the Chimney Rock National Monument falls from mid-May to mid-September, due to funding constraints as well as the seasonal challenges of the location. Today, visitors can enjoy guided or self-guided tours on the Chimney Rock Mesa. In addition, during the course of the summer season, volunteers present a number of special events on topics such as archaeology, archaeoastronomy, astronomy, geology, plants, and tribal ceremonies. (Courtesy of the authors' collection.)

Today, CRIA manages Chimney Rock National Monument on a day-to-day basis. Volunteers and paid staff—including day manager Shelleah Conitchan (left), mesa monitor Alice Firestone (middle), and tour guide Lyniss Steinert (right)—participate in the daily operations of the monument. (Courtesy of the authors' collection.)

Today, volunteers of CRIA provide educational tours and special programs on astronomy and pottery. They also support local schools and tribal ceremonies. CRIA is granted an annual special use permit by the US Forest Service to provide these activities and to help with both monitoring and stabilizing efforts. From left to right, CRIA volunteers Dick Bond, Sandy Billings, and Herb Billings welcome visitors from inside Raby Cabin. (Courtesy of the authors' collection.)

For the past 25 years, archaeologists and scholars of Four Corners culture and history have identified Chimney Rock as an outlier community of Chaco Canyon. Evidence of this connection includes pottery, architecture, and communication networks. Although much discussion exists regarding interpretations of specific resources, the connection that Chimney Rock exhibits with the rest of the ancient Southwest is undisputed. However, what does Chimney Rock mean to professional scholars, local residents, and regional tribes? Something different, certainly, but similarities overlap. It is in this overlap that one finds the core principle of its identity. The resources were protected and named by Congress as a settlement under the Chaco Outliers Protection Act of 1995. In September 2012, Pres. Barack Obama proclaimed it Chimney Rock National Monument. (Courtesy of US Forest Service, Pagosa District.)

BIBLIOGRAPHY

Chimney Rock National Monument. www.chimneyrockco.org

Eddy, Frank W. *Archaeological Investigations at Chimney Rock Mesa: 1970–1972.* Boulder, CO: Colorado Archaeological Society, 1977.

Hands of Time Volunteer Training Handbook. Pagosa Springs, CO: Chimney Rock Interpretive Association, 2013.

Houle, Marcy C. *Wings for My Flight: The Peregrine Falcons of Chimney Rock.* Boulder, CO: Pruett Publishing, 1999.

Jeancon, Jean Allard. *Archaeological Research in the Northeastern San Juan Basin of Colorado During the Summer of 1921.* Denver, CO: The State Historical and Natural History Society of Colorado and the University of Denver, 1922.

Lekson, Stephen H. *A History of the Ancient Southwest.* Santa Fe, NM: School for Advanced Research Press, 2008.

Lister, Florence C. *In The Shadow of the Rocks: Archaeology of the Chimney Rock District in Southwest Colorado.* Durango, CO: Durango Herald Small Press, 2011.

Malville, J. McKim. *A Guide to Prehistoric Astronomy in the Southwest.* Boulder, CO: 3D Press, 2012.

———, ed. *Chimney Rock: The Ultimate Outlier.* Lanham, MD: Lexington Books, 2004.

Mysterious Chimney Rock: The Land, The Sky, The People. Colorado Historical Society and Chimney Rock Interpretive Association, 2006.

Raby, Glenn. *From the Bottom of the Ocean to the Top of the World (…and Everything in Between): The Geology of Pagosa Country.* Pagosa Springs, CO: San Juan National Forest and BLM Public Lands, 2008.

Renaud, E.B. (Etienne Bernardeau). *Field Notes: 1st Expedition Summer 1921 Piedra Parada and 2nd Expedition Summer 1922.* Unpublished manuscript housed at University of Denver, Department of Anthropology, Special Collections.

Richardson, Helen L., ed. *Visions of Chimney Rock: A Photographic Interpretation of the Place and Its People.* Montrose, CO: Western Reflections Publishing Company, 2006.

Roberts, Frank H.H. *Early Pueblo Ruins in the Piedra District, Southwestern Colorado. Bureau of American Ethnology Bulletin 96.* Washington, DC: Smithsonian Institution, 1930.

Sutcliffe, Ron. *Moon Tracks: A Guide to Understanding Some of the Patterns We See with an Emphasis on Southwest Ancient Puebloan Cultures.* Pagosa Springs, CO: Moonspiral Press, 2006.

INDEX

Note: Includes only persons identified in images

DISCOVER THOUSANDS OF LOCAL HISTORY BOOKS FEATURING MILLIONS OF VINTAGE IMAGES

Arcadia Publishing, the leading local history publisher in the United States, is committed to making history accessible and meaningful through publishing books that celebrate and preserve the heritage of America's people and places.

Find more books like this at
www.arcadiapublishing.com

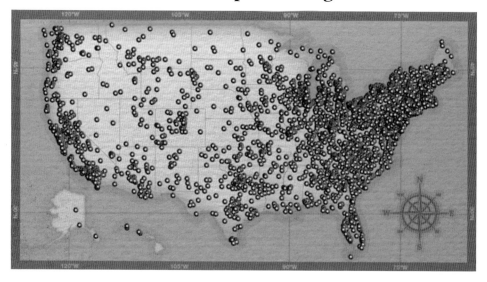

Search for your hometown history, your old stomping grounds, and even your favorite sports team.

Consistent with our mission to preserve history on a local level, this book was printed in South Carolina on American-made paper and manufactured entirely in the United States. Products carrying the accredited Forest Stewardship Council (FSC) label are printed on 100 percent FSC-certified paper.

MADE IN THE

USA